THE
ORDER
OF A

Son

DEVELOPING *the*
UNIQUE RELATIONSHIP
BETWEEN MINISTRY FATHERS
and SONS

THE
ORDER
OF A

Son

DEVELOPING *the*
UNIQUE RELATIONSHIP
BETWEEN MINISTRY FATHERS
and SONS

DR. MARK HANBY
with ROGER ROTH

Destiny Image₀ Publishers, Inc.
P.O. Box 310
Shippensburg, PA 17257-0310

"Speaking to the Purposes of God for This Generation
and for the Generations to Come"

ISBN 0-7684-2304-X

For Worldwide Distribution
Printed in the U.S.A.

This book and all other Destiny Image, Revival Press, MercyPlace, Fresh Bread, Destiny Image Fiction, and Treasure House books are available at Christian bookstores and distributors worldwide.

1 2 3 4 5 6 7 8 9 10 / 09 08 07 06 05

For a U.S. bookstore nearest you, call **1-800-722-6774**.
For more information on foreign distributors, call **717-532-3040**.
Or reach us on the Internet:
www.destinyimage.com

CONTENTS

PREFACE

S ince the publication of *You Have Not Many Fathers* in 1996, thousands in ministry and numerous churches world-wide have been forever changed by its contents. A flood of testimonials, from clergy and laity alike, continue to attest to ministries and lives that have found order and direction and have been transformed by its teachings. Due to this outpouring it became apparent that there was a great need for a sequel to discuss how to pass on father/son order to ministry sons and implement these teachings in a church setting.

The book, *You Have Not Many Fathers*, discusses what is perhaps the most powerful and important message for the Church in our day. In a systematic and insightful way, it uses the Word of God to show what the biblical order of fathers and sons is. It also discusses why the reestablishment of such order is essential for the fulfillment of God's purpose in our lives and in the Church as a whole.

Through biblical patterns and personal revelation, the author not only helps the Church understand its present anemic position but also defines the restoration of godly order that will bring the Church to its completed purpose. As a result of this pioneering work and the clear purpose and call of the Spirit, the spiritual necessity of coming into father/son order has become evident to many.

You Have Not Many Fathers answered the question about what father/son order is; whereas this book seeks to answer questions as to how this order can be brought to pass in the local church. How can Church leaders and heads of local churches take what is so foundational to God's plan and make it practical in their settings? How can those in ministry teach father/son order in a clear and systematic way in the local church?

How can it be taught in such a way that it will not only be accepted but also applied? Of equal importance, how can those in a position of oversight help it become a lifestyle and not just a doctrine? As all in leadership are so keenly aware, there is a vast difference between having people accept a teaching and having them conform their lives to that teaching.

In the past few years and through a number of avenues, the Lord has brought various pastors and church heads in contact with the topic of father/son relationships. The interchanges with these various leaders can be summed up in the same question: "How can father/son order become a reality in my church?" Many also said: "I believe and understand the necessity of establishing these relationships within my congregation—they've changed my life—but how can I bring my church into this order?"

It has become apparent that not only do church leaders need materials to help their local churches understand father/son relationships, but they themselves need to understand that there is an order and pattern as to how this revelation can be ministered and received by the church. To this end the following chapters have been devoted to helping church leadership understand the process of bringing this desired order to their local settings.

What follows is born out of a quest for biblical relationships in ministry. It is the result of father/son order ministered by the Spirit to many pastors who have witnessed the ability of this order to empower and revitalize their ministries and churches. Those who have experienced the blessing of father/son order are ever cognizant of the favor and grace of the Lord that is imparted to us through this relationship.

An increasing number of Church leaders are realizing that in order for their vision and purpose—given to them by God—to survive their lifetime, it must become generational. However, they are at a loss as to how to implement this biblical order.

That is the reason for this book. Springing from lessons learned in local churches as well as questions and problems raised by various pastors, the information in this book will assist the local church and its leaders to be brought into biblical father/son order.

INTRODUCTION

*M*ost of *us* who reside in America are of ancestral stock with origins in distant lands. These stout-hearted people were drawn to this land for various reasons. Some wanted to escape persecution; others were seeking opportunity; but most had, as a central part of their hope, a desire to dwell in a land that would provide security, well-being, and freedom to succeeding generations.

Like these stalwart pioneers, so we in Christianity are on a journey from a temporary land fraught with turmoil to a permanent land of promise.

In the heart of many of these courageous immigrants was the desire to give to the next generation more than had been given to them. There was a willingness to endure extreme sacrifice so that their sons and daughters might have a better inheritance.

In the present-day attitude of self-interest, responsibility for the next generation has largely been abandoned, and with it goes the possibility of a progressive future. In many places it is more likely that the next generation will be aborted than that it will be raised to live in its full potential. Unfortunately the natural environment corresponds with the spiritual condition of the Church.

Generally the church world is not interested in the sacrifice that is required to raise up a better generation. Not only do they not

13

want to invest the time and commitment required, but also they know that giving another generation an inheritance would interfere with the material and social pursuits of the church. Many in ministry are far more likely to castrate sons than to give them double portions. It is a spirit that is consumed by "self" and "now," thus devoid of future and purpose. God, however, is overturning these materialistic tables and calling forth a remnant whose hearts again will be set in right order.

Like Abraham, we seek a city built and made by the hand of God. As we learn from Joshua, true leadership desires to lead the people of God to the inheritance in the land the Lord swore to give Israel. As the psalmist David did, the mature sons of God ask, *"How shall we sing the Lord's song in a strange land?"*[1] Father/son order is the process by which we make the journey from the strange land of religious bondage to Zion, the land of fulfilled promise.

The Need to Carry This Order to Future Generations

> *In His humiliation His judgment was taken away: and who shall declare His generation? for His life is taken from the earth.*[2]

In the above Scripture, the Ethiopian eunuch is trying to understand who it was that Isaiah was speaking about. Philip began at this Scripture and preached unto him Jesus. This led to the pronouncement from the eunuch, *"I believe that Jesus Christ is the Son of God."*[3]

All that Philip told him about Jesus—of His ministry, of His power, of His miracles, of His death and resurrection—was summed up in one brief statement of belief that spoke of Jesus' relationship with a father: *"Jesus Christ is the Son of God."*[4] It is impossible to understand Jesus' ministry, and it is impractical to think we will be able to understand our own ministries, without comprehending biblical sonship.

Isaiah asks, "*Who shall declare his generation?*"[5] It is a question left for us to answer. Who is the generation of Jesus? From where do His descendants come? Who will bring forth the knowledge of the generation of Christ in the earth?

Only those who understand and follow biblical father/son relationship can comprehend the generation of Christ that will bring the appearing of Jesus to the world. Only those who understand the absolute necessity of replicating their ministries in future generations will be able to pass on inheritance. We in ministry should not be marking the effectiveness of our ministries by what we have been able to accomplish but by whether or not we have been able to successfully pass down the inheritance, given by God, to the next generation.

Those of us who are reaching for father/son order in our ministries have come to understand the absolute importance of such relationships to the furtherance of our particular callings. We need, however, to see the broader context of how this order might be carried throughout all the generations. It was not merely entrusted to us for our personal benefit. More importantly, each of us is a link in this order to bring forth the completion of the Church and the manifestation of the Kingdom.

What God is doing cannot be completed in any one generation. We are all parts in the purpose of God's plan to bring forth restoration. Many have been taught to look for their success in Jesus in all the wrong places. Success in ministry should not be measured by amount of gifting, building projects, size of congregations, or by the measure of influence we have over others.

If we are going to gauge success at all, let us do it as Jesus did. He measured His accomplishment in fulfilling His purpose, "*It is finished*," and in preparing the next generation, "*Of them which Thou gavest Me have I lost none.*"[6] Jesus did many mighty miracles, preached to thousands, walked perfectly in the gifts, yet the witness of all these would have died at Calvary except for the fact that He prepared another generation in the Apostles to carry on the vision.

> *Neither shall thy name any more be called Abram, but thy name shall be Abraham; for a father of many nations have I made thee.*[7]

> *For I know him, that he will command his children and his household after him, and they shall keep the way of the Lord, to do justice and judgment; that the Lord may bring upon Abraham that which He hath spoken of him.*[8]

> *The Angel which redeemed me from all evil, bless the lads; and let my name be named on them, and the name of my fathers Abraham and Isaac; and let them grow into a multitude in the midst of the earth.*[9]

The fathers of Israel—Abraham, Isaac, and Jacob—show us the pattern for what the Lord desires to do in father/son relationships. They demonstrate the need to carry ministry to the third and fourth generation and plainly show the necessity of establishing order to the fourth generation if the plan of God is ever going to be fulfilled in the Church. To that foundation I would like to add some insights that hopefully will help us understand the absolute necessity of establishing biblical father/son order.

The Lord made great promises to Abraham. He would be the father of many nations and the progenitor of innumerable descendants. So great were the promises and the faith of this man that God, through our faith in Christ, makes Abraham our ancestor. "*And if ye be Christ's, then are ye Abraham's seed, and heirs according to the promise.*"[10]

Abraham was the inheritor of great promises but he was totally dependent upon his offspring to bring them to pass. God could promise him a great name and a great lineage but only sons in order would have the ability to make those promises become a reality. This is why part of what constituted the faith of Abraham was his willingness to put his sons and house in order.

> *For I know him, that he will command his children and his household after him, and they shall keep the way of the Lord...that the Lord may bring upon Abraham that which He hath spoken of him.*[11]

God knew that Abraham would be able to pass on to his children the things the Lord had given him. This is one reason He could make such great promises to Abraham. God must also know this about us if we are to establish father/son order throughout the generations.

For the Lord to bring upon us the things He has spoken, He requires us to command sons who will carry on in the ministry and vision He has given us. Being able to command children carries with it the same directive given Timothy, to *"commit to faithful men"*[12] the things he had heard from Paul. There must be a passing on of the father's ministry. Each generation has a distinct mission but it must expand on the foundation and purpose of the preceding generation.

Abraham could only be the father of a multitude if he had a son who would carry on his vision and seed. If Isaac had refused, then the promise would have died with Abraham and God would have had to choose another to fulfill His purpose. If Abraham had failed to produce understanding and desire in his son, then the promise of God could not have gone beyond Abraham's generation.

In His foreknowledge, God knew that Abraham would *"command his children after him."*[13] It was not just Isaac upon which Abraham had to trust but upon Isaac's children. Isaac not only had to give birth to another generation, but he also had to instill in that generation the vision of his father.

17

This Isaac was able to do. Are we as ministers of this dispensation able to do likewise? When God looks at us in ministry, He is not only looking for how we will answer the call given to us, but also for how we will pass on to others the things we have been given. It is one thing for a father to teach a son how to be a father; it is quite another to teach a son how to teach a third generation to be a father.

There have been many great men and women throughout the ages of Christendom who were anointed and chosen by God, yet their vision, rather than geometrically multiplying into future generations, died upon their death. Instead of being starting points from which spiritual revelation and order might reproduce and flourish in successive generations, their ministries usually ended with followers building religious organizations giving testimony of what God had done through these individuals. The reason for this is that although they may have had a great call in God, they never learned to raise up sons. They had many followers but no legitimate sons who could receive inheritance and also knew how to pass on inheritance.

We must learn to think generationally. In the Bible, a person's identity and purpose could not be separated from his ancestry and offspring. Who your forefathers were and what your descendants would become were of utmost importance. In the church world, neither the establishing of identity and purpose in sons nor the passing on of inheritance seem to be of any great desire or consequence.

It is not too strong of a statement to say that a ministry that fails to pass on inheritance to sons is a ministry that has failed to complete its purpose in Christ. We have a great opportunity in this day to break the generational curses that have for so long plagued the church. We have the opportunity to restore the foundations of many generations.

The curse on the church world is a curse of immaturity due to a loss of excellence. Most of us have learned from the biblical admonition about following boy leaders instead of fathers.

For though ye have ten thousand instructors [boy teachers] in Christ, yet have ye not many fathers: for in Christ Jesus I have begotten you through the gospel.[14]

This immaturity has caused the Church to live in single portions of God's blessing and purpose rather than in the double portions of inheritance. We in ministry must learn that for all our accomplishments, unless we are able to pass on inheritance to sons, most of our work dies with us. This lack of understanding leaves to following generations the responsibility to lay again beginning foundations that have been destroyed and rebuilt many times.

The great blessing of inheritance is that the one who receives inheritance acquires without cost or effort that which others have fought and labored to gain. The doctrines of justification by faith and supremacy of the Word that caused many reformers great opposition, and in some cases cost them their lives, have cost those of us who have inherited the fruits of their great struggles nothing but our willingness to believe and implement them.

They passed on foundations upon which others could build. Those of us who have learned to become true fathers have the ability to pass on the same type of inheritance to our sons. What cost us much can be freely added to them. What we have received out of the depth of our struggle and commitment to follow the voice of God over the shouts of men becomes theirs because of relationship. The Lord, because of relationship, gives them a double blessing by adding what He has given us to what He is giving them. Our hearts must be turned toward our sons.

For ye remember, brethren, our labor and travail: for laboring night and day, because we would not be chargeable unto any of you, we preached unto you the gospel of God. Ye are witnesses, and God also, how holily and justly and unblameably we behaved ourselves among you that believe: As ye know how we exhorted and comforted and charged every one of you, as a father doth his children, that ye would walk worthy of God, who hath called you unto His kingdom and glory.[15]

ENDNOTES

1. Psalm 137:4.
2. Acts 8:33.
3. Acts 8:37.
4. Acts 8:37.
5. Isaiah 53:8.
6. John 19:30; 18:9.
7. Genesis 17:5.
8. Genesis 18:19.
9. Genesis 48:16.
10. Galatians 3:29.
11. Genesis 18:19.
12. See Second Timothy 2:2.
13. See Genesis 18:19.
14. 1 Corinthians 4:15.
15. 1 Thessalonians 2:9-12.

CHAPTER ONE

FATHER/SON ORDER AS A TOOL FOR DISCIPLESHIP

The implementation of father/son order offers the assurance of not only impacting the lost but also discipling every saint. This is an assurance that no other method, past or present, has been able to accomplish. Today there are approximately six billion people in the world. That is an almost unfathomable number.

It is impossible in any one lifetime to know even a small fraction of those living, yet the Lord knows each of us intimately and with far greater understanding than even we know ourselves. We are at the time in history when the number of people alive today exceeds the number of people who have ever lived upon this earth. The earth is fast approaching six billion human inhabitants. These are numbers that stretch the mind's ability to comprehend.

We can picture a thousand. We can possibly grasp a million. It is almost beyond our mental abilities however to accurately appreciate numbers that reach into the billions. The following may perhaps provide some help in this area.

Understanding a Population of Six Billion

To speak just the first name of a billion people would take a person over 30 years, speaking one new name per second, 24 hours a day. At this rate, to complete the roll of the names of each person on earth would take a continuous 180+ years.

The last 10,000 minutes of our life cover about a week. The last 100,000 minutes would take us back about two and a half months. A million minutes ago would find us back in time almost two years. Were we able to travel back in time a billion minutes we would find ourselves alive at the time of the first-century church.

If we think about a billion in terms of money, we could use the following comparisons to understand how large a billion is. A billion dollars would be enough to build 250 elementary schools. A billion dollars would be enough to give every man, woman, and child in Madison, Wisconsin, or Chattanooga, Tennessee, $5,000. It would be enough to give 10,000 families a yearly salary of $100,000, or it would be enough to give 50,000 people a new first class automobile.

One billion is a lot, and yet there are over six billion people in the world today. Not only that, but at the current rate that number will increase in the next 50 years to over nine billion people. Many modern evangelical and Bible churches are continually theorizing, even sometimes agonizing, over how to reach such vast numbers of people with the gospel.

Traditional Approaches

Numerous traditional churches have solved this perplexity by broadening their definition of salvation to include all "good" people of all religions—a kind of "many ways to God" mentality. Others excitedly look for methods and approaches that can reach increased numbers of people. All of course thank God for any who come into relationship with Jesus Christ.

If we searched the Scripture we would see that it is God who adds to the church daily *"such as should be saved."*[1] God does have a plan. It is a plan built on His order and not our good intentions or perplexity about reaching the lost. Some in the Church have forgotten that although the saints have an important role to play in reaching the world, it is the Lord who saves, not us, and He never fails.

Important Questions

Is there not a disparity and a contradiction in a church world seeking the salvation of the lost but not seeking its own sanctification and order with the same zeal and purpose? What if the salvation of a lost world was somehow tied to the Church's coming into biblical order? What if their salvation was not so much dependent on evangelism methods as on the Church's willingness to change and follow principles long contained in Scripture?

Yet what vehicle can possibly reach the growing mass of humanity needing God, and not only reach them, but according to His command, disciple them as well? Could it be that if the Church were willing to submit itself to the order of the Spirit, it would have no difficulty in accomplishing every task given it by the Lord? Is it possible that the Lord has no problem saving the lost but has difficulty, so to speak, with a Church that is unwilling or unknowledgeable in ordering itself after the Spirit?

God, I believe, is dealing with our lack of understanding, our prejudice and shortsightedness, as to what the Church of God is and what and who constitute the local assembly. If we look even curtly at our local churches, we can readily see some things we do in the way of organization and worship that are done purely because of tradition or our human desire to do good things for God.

Perhaps we have been lulled by our good intentions into being inattentive, without a proper regard for understanding the biblical order or premise for all we seek to do. What if we found we were doing good things for God that He never told us to do? Would this realization change our approach, and in what ways?

Past and Present Approaches to "Soul Winning"

It comes as a surprise to many that the average paying membership of a local church Body, not visitors, is less than 100. Yet the professed goal of most church bodies would be the salvation of their cities and indeed the entire world. Indeed the average church focuses on "soul winning."

There have been many methods to "win the lost" throughout the history of Christianity, which have met with a varied amount of success. Most have involved the establishment of Church systems— a few, at times, even resorting to physical force and warfare on the part of some to "save the world for Christ." The evangelism movement that grew out of the Reformation has been actively employed in one form or another for several hundred years yet has failed to reach the entire world or even a large portion thereof.

In this past century the Pentecostal and Charismatic movements have reached large numbers of people. Even these, however, using the promise of the gifts and power of the Holy Spirit through faith as a means of reaching the lost, have come nowhere close to achieving this purpose. Likewise, Evangelical church systems have been important vehicles for reaching many people. Many have employed methods of revivals, Word training, or massive outreaches through crusades with significant results, yet all have fallen far short of reaching the world for Christ.

There have, in some ways, been benefits from these evangelistic efforts, and without doubt there have been many who have come to know the Lord. This is, of course, a very good thing. Yet to even the most optimistic eye, the Church has not come close to approximating even the effect of the early Church, much less reaching the entire world with the gospel. Some, it seems, have resigned themselves to believing that what we are experiencing, with all its glaring inconsistencies, is the promised move of God.

Many see the Church as being past its zenith with only the harsh judgment of God yet to be unleashed. Others believe that God, in a fashion, will just snap His divine fingers and supernaturally bring to pass what the effort of the entire church age has been unable to produce. Almost all hope for a great move in the earth toward redemption before the long anticipated coming of judgment from God.

Every year 78,000,000 more people are born than die. The Church is in no way even keeping pace with the birth rate. For the Church just to keep pace would require the salvation of a city larger than Cincinnati, Ohio, or Kansas City, Missouri, each week and this would do nothing to reach the billions yet untouched by the gospel.

The majority of pastors dream of shepherding a church with a thousand members and never see it. The small number who pastor churches of 2,000 or more (so-called "mega-churches"), usually do so as a result of great personal sacrifice. All who give their hearts to the people of God in feeding and nurturing the saints of God are deserving of honor and the reward of God.

If, however, we leave our prejudices and personal desires behind and look objectively and openly at the circumstance of the modern church, we might gain some important understanding. We might come to understand that nowhere in Scripture has the responsibility for winning a city been laid solely on the shoulders of the pastor. More importantly, we might see that none of our efforts or plans, as beneficial as they may be, have won or will win the world for Christ. *Most* importantly, we might see that God is capable of bringing to pass all that is spoken by His own power.

In truth, we are not helping God, but it is He who is helping us! We might then come to understand that we aren't winning the world for Christ, but He is allowing us to participate in and reap the blessing of all that He is doing. It then becomes a question not of what we are doing for Christ but what He will do for and through us if we are willing to come into divine order.

Ministry Multiplication

Now suppose a man of God were able to build a church of 10,000 members—a feat that only a very small fraction have been able to achieve. Such an effort, if accomplished in God, is indeed significant and worthy of proper recognition. To achieve this would not only require great effort but the help of many loyal and dedicated men and women, not to mention the provision and grace of God to keep it holy and God-centered.

If someone were to do this, we would consider it a great and marvelous achievement, and rightfully so. But do we realize that, as great as this might be, if it were not established in father/son order it would pale by comparison to a ministry that has been able to rear only a few or even just one son in proper order?

A local church of thousands, if not founded on father/son order, will never perpetually continue in the vision and purpose to which God called its founder. This is not to say that it will not be "Christian" or do "good" things, but it will, in time, become religious, not continuing in the vision by which it was brought forth. Many churches that started out in vision doing "God things" have, in their inability to increase in order, resorted to doing "good things."

The preponderance of historical evidence speaks this fact loudly and clearly for all ministries to hear: "Only sons in right order will carry on ministry." Even a brief look at present-day Christian religions shows a wide discrepancy between the vision, call, and doctrine of their original founders and the practice of those organizations that claim their fatherhood.

A man whom God uses to build a church of 10,000 does a good thing for those who have been touched by his ministry. But most of the work he does will never continue as intended by God if his ministry is not built upon proper father/son order. It cannot be merely a pattern of mentoring but needs to be one of father/son order. If not, that ministry will never become generational, and others in the future will have to dig wells and build walls destroyed by immaturity and neglect because of the lack of proper order.

Only a father in ministry can pass on the full measure of identity, purpose, inheritance, vision, and blessing. To have a church of 10,000, if done in God, is a good thing, but to have just one son in proper order is better and of more lasting importance. To understand this, church leaders would have to become servants to the saints. They would have to understand that God's purpose is not vested in the work of their own hands but in the future generations.

Let's suppose that the founder of a church of 10,000 goes on to be with the Lord without instilling proper father/son order in the church. To the religious and the world at large it is considered a great ministry. The thousands of lives touched, the buildings dedicated to godly uses, and the programs that met the needs of many all testify to that ministry's effect.

The failure to establish father/son order would, however, guarantee that that church will eventually fall victim to religious methods, loss of vision, and continual immaturity unless and until some future leader brings forth the order that is lacking. To be Christ-focused is to be focused on the future generations. *"For the joy that was set before Him endured the cross."*[2]

Jesus' ministry was for all generations and the redemptive future, not about His personal notoriety or the masses of people drawn to Him. Isn't it interesting that our attempts to win the lost often coincide with our efforts to increase numbers, ministerial influence, building programs, and financial position? Jesus' focus was beyond His ministry. All too often our focus is our ministry.

Now let's suppose that another minister with a much smaller (in the sense of numbers and religious recognition) ministry also goes to be with the Lord. However, this pastor, unlike the previous example, had successfully raised sons in ministry who learned to walk in proper order. His work, though initially small (in number and size), will continue to grow in subsequent generations and the vision given through him will grow by the maturity and order of his sons. In a short time it will far surpass the other ministry in both size and lasting effect.

This can be likened to Jesus' use of the parable of the mustard seed. *"The kingdom of heaven is like to a grain of mustard seed, which a man took, and sowed in his field: Which indeed is the least of all seeds: but when it is grown, it is the greatest among herbs, and becometh a tree, so that the birds of the air come and lodge in the branches thereof."*[3]

It's because a man of God sowed the seed of this order into sons that the ministry and vision given him by God will continue to grow and become established even after his physical death.

Every ministry involves more than just the rearing of ministry sons. The call and vision become the field of our spiritual work and provide a workplace and training opportunity for the ministry sons given from the Lord. Jesus established a work that was passed on to the disciples. His ministry was, in part, a training ground for the disciples, and its continuation after His death became a significant part of their purpose.

The proper establishment of father/son order is the only way that the gospel of the Kingdom will be preached in the entire world. It's not the gospel, as defined by some, but the gospel of the Kingdom that will be preached in all the world. All the world may not follow after Jesus in our day, but all the world will be given a witness of the gospel of the Kingdom. There is, of course, a day coming when His Kingdom will be established forever but this is dependent on the generations coming into order.

This is one reason why father/son order is the only tool that is able to disciple the entire church. Let's suppose that a minister is not only interested in reaching the lost but in bringing forth ministry sons—if, for example, a minister was given just ten people in his whole ministry and he took those ten and established with them a father/son relationship.

If he were to do as Paul instructed and as Abraham demonstrated and as Jesus accomplished by His example, and commit ministry to *"faithful men, who shall be able to teach others also,"*[4] so that they likewise would have ministry relationship with just ten others who would themselves do likewise, do you know that within 12 years that ministry, which started with just that one man, would have grown to 10,000 people—people who are not only saints but disciples—and that in only 18 years that ministry would have reached 1,000,000 disciples? Within 30 years the entire population of the earth could be not only saved but discipled—if all were willing to turn toward the Lord.

The most likely reason that this does not happen is because relationship takes time and emptying of self. The Church today is ministry-conscious, not relationship-conscious. It is result-oriented, not life-changing. To have purposeful, meaningful, intimate relationship with even ten people limits time, opportunity, and availability to do "mass ministry." The biblical plan will require a rethinking and reordering of how we understand ministry and the purpose of the Church. God has begun this reordering, and though it will be opposed by some, it will forever change how ministry functions and how the lost are reached with the gospel.

Order is a hard thing for people to grasp because it involves preparation, time, and change on the part of those who would enter such order. The Lord is not going to establish a new method for either reaching the lost or for bringing the Church into maturity. The methods existent within His Word are just as capable of achieving His purposes today as when first written. The life of Jesus is a pattern, the ministry of Paul is a pattern, and even the Word itself is a pattern to be followed.

The problem for the Church is not the need to devise new methods of outreach or organization but rather the need to understand and follow the patterns already established by God. For ministry, godly father/son order is the only way to fully accomplish the call.

ENDNOTES

1. Acts 2:47.
2. Hebrews 12:2.
3. Matthew 13:31-32.
4. 2 Timothy 2:2.

CHAPTER TWO

PREPARATION OF
THE SET MINISTRY

*T*he *heart* of ministry must be turned toward raising sons and passing on inheritance. There is a preparation, however, that is necessary for this process to be effective and for it to become continuous in our spiritual descendants. We are not born as completely functioning fathers full of wisdom, with developed paternal instincts, nor were we perfect in our walk as sons. We required correction, direction, and growth to become vessels fit for service to a father. In Christ we are always in a state of becoming. This speaks of change, this speaks of process, and this speaks of a need for preparation.

> *To turn the hearts of the fathers to the children...to make ready a **people prepared** for the Lord.*[1]

> *So the service of the house of the Lord was set in order...God had **prepared the people**: for the thing was done suddenly.*[2]

Fathers and sons need to be prepared. The quick or sudden work the Lord is doing on our watch is the result of coming into

His divine order. To believe or understand a doctrine is one thing; to implement it in our churches is quite another.

As we mature in ministry we realize that for the most part our churches are really a reflection of our ministries. Our weaknesses as ministers, our fears that follow us like a fiend prowling in the shadows, our immaturity in certain areas that we shield from our eyes, and even our lack of understanding usually show up as symptoms in our congregations. Praise be to God for understanding that frees us from the curse of immaturity!

We sometimes fight and struggle with our congregations, weep and plead before the Lord. At times we complain and give vent to our frustrations in an effort to change our churches into what we understand they should become. Yet in one way, they are really just a mirror that gives reflection to the character and the maturity of our ministries. As they reflect inconsistencies and weakness in our ministries, either we can lash out at the symptoms or we can allow the Spirit to bring change to us that will allow growth in them.

If we truly want to bring maturity and perfection to our churches, we must prepare ourselves to be fathers mature enough to pass on inheritance. We must see our need and be willing to allow the Lord to prepare us as skillful fathers adept at bringing forth mature sons. Growth cannot come without change. Order cannot come without preparation.

Defining the Set Minister's Responsibility

God has set in each properly ordered local church a minister to establish and oversee the work. This minister, usually called the "pastor," is not the owner of the church. He is not necessarily the wisest or most spiritual of all the members in the congregation. His spiritual gifting in certain areas may not even approach that of many in the faithful sainthood.

The set minister cannot be all things to all people; he must not view himself or be viewed as the repository of all knowledge or the one who has the answer to every need in every situation. He is, however, the only one, because of the position entrusted to his care, who can minister an order that will complete God's vision for a particular local Body.

The set minister, in his position to establish and oversee the work of the local church, must institute proper order. More than any other single task, bringing the church into proper father/son order must define his ministry. A ministry without this order, which defines itself by its size, influence, or gifting, will remain an inadequate and half-grown ministry at best.

Ministerial *responsibility* is the ability to provide proper response to those issues related to our ministries. The difference between reacting to a situation and responding to one can be vast. When someone reacts, they allow circumstances to dictate their actions and attitudes; when someone responds, they allow their attitudes and actions to be controlled by an ordered and developed character.

Many in ministry find themselves constantly reacting to "problems." Sometimes a minister may find himself in the position of continually putting out fires within the church. No sooner does he deal with one situation than another arises. This creates a position of stress that can annul the peace of God.

The ministry oftentimes finds itself continually reacting (having to act again) because it defaults in its responsibility to set proper father/son order throughout the generations of the church. Learning to properly respond and establishing an order within the church that allows response to the Spirit rather than reaction to opposition is one of the primary responsibilities of the set ministry.

The set ministry is a ministry of leadership. That means that it must know where the Lord wants it to go and how to get there. This requires a clear godly vision that can be imparted to the church. The set minister is responsible for the effective operation of the church. This means that he must establish the church upon the government of God and not upon that of man.

The set ministry is responsible for how and what the church is taught. This requires sound doctrine and grounding in the truth. The set ministry is responsible for the training of ministry and the completion of church order. This requires the establishment of biblical father/son order.

The Need to Desire Sons

It is impossible to establish the complete order of God for the church without first desiring sons. Immature ministry does not crave sons but followers. A mark of youth is that it seeks material reward and friendship over responsibility. The fullest measure of maturity in ministry is to take on the responsibility of maturing sons.

Undeveloped ministries desire an entourage of youthful followers in place of sons. It is more edifying to the flesh and less work. To raise sons requires a labor of love. It requires a confidence in one's own ministry and a lack of fear from competition as others in the church grow in the revelation and power of the Lord.

The attitude of a true father is that he wants his sons to have all the Lord desires for them. In addition, he wants the things that he as a father has received from God to be given to the sons as well. This produces double-portion rather than single-portion ministries. This requires the passing on of inheritance; it requires a willingness to take those things of value that belong to me and give them to another because of relationship.

There must be an understanding that all things given to me by God are temporary and that the majority of my work in the Lord will not last unless it becomes generational. Immaturity can only see the now; maturity sees the eternity. In order to administer father/son order, a minister must be able to see and think generationally and be willing to bestow all his inheritance in God on sons.

> *But Jesus called them unto him, and said, Ye know that the princes of the Gentiles exercise dominion over them, and they that are great exercise authority upon them. But it shall not be so among you: but whosoever will be great among you, let him be your minister; and whosoever will be chief among you, let him be your servant: Even as the Son of man came not to be ministered unto, but to minister, and to give His life a ransom for many.*[3]

A ministry father must lead by example. There are many fatherless sons calling for relationship with a true father. The heart of the father must be turned toward the son; it is the father's choosing and responsibility. The father's purpose must not be the promotion of self but the furtherance of the vision in his sons.

He must be willing to teach them how to walk in the kingdom by putting the work of God ahead of their personal feelings and ambitions. He should desire ministry toward sons over the ministry from sons, since *"Even the Son of man came not to be ministered unto, but to minister."*[4] Many seek followers; but ministries desiring relationship seek sons.

Ulterior Motives in Fathering

In establishing father/son order in a local church the set minister should allow the Spirit to reveal hidden motives for desiring such order. Some who try to teach this truth do it from self-seeking and self-serving agendas and not out of a desire to give inheritance or to raise sons. Among the multitudes of ministries there are few with the maturity to put the welfare of sons above the pursuit of personal ministry.

Unscrupulous ministers have found that teaching modifications of this order is a good way to increase income and to demand tithe and compliance from those they call sons. Others suffer from trying to be God substitutes for their congregations. The teaching of father/son order by unprincipled pastors in immature congregations is an effective way to demand allegiance and to wrongfully elevate the clergy over the saints. Still other leaders who are out of order use portions of this teaching to support their disorder.

It is not enough to desire sons, but fathers must also be willing to raise sons. A ministry father's heart must be given over to that purpose or the trials and adversities will precipitately abort the process. Those longing to instill proper father/son order in their churches must check for ulterior motives. Proper order is dependent on a right heart.

In the course of our ministries we have all come to experience the hand of God channeling our work into more productive areas. Every true minister of the Lord has received chastisement to bring him into fuller alignment with the will of God. All of us know the voice of God revealing things about ourselves that were hidden from our eyes.

His grace and mercy have many times made up for our weaknesses. He will continue to perfect us if we are willing to remain on the potter's wheel as He reveals our true nature to us; "*that thou hide not thyself from thine own flesh.*"[5] Although it is sometimes painful, understanding ulterior motives helps free us from our flesh.

The Need to Be Following a Father

The following of man is so prevalent within modern Christianity that we need to be clear in understanding what is meant by following a ministry father. God is our Father. Ultimately, He is the one we need to serve. A father in ministry is not a substitute or a mediator for our heavenly Father. Misunderstanding this key point is a mark of immature relationships and not of those who are in proper father/son order.

Father/son relationship is not the order of our personal relationship with the Lord. Father/son order pertains to the order within ministry. There is no intermediary in our personal relationship with the Lord. It needs to be a personal relationship between God and us. We can witness to the lost, hear God, grow in love with Him, heal the sick, and "go to Heaven" all without being in proper father/son order. The reason is that these things are born out of our personal relationship with God.

Father/son relationship is the order that relates to ministry. To understand and receive proper vision, to find true identity, to complete our full purpose and to receive our entire biblical inheritance requires this order. It is not the following of a man but the establishment of a God-ordained order. It is His plan for the bringing forth of Kingdom ministry. We can live as Christians without this order but we can never fulfill His full purpose unless we learn to become connected to it.

For even Christ pleased not Himself; but as it is written,
The reproaches of them that reproached Thee fell on Me.[6]

In following a father in ministry we gain many valuable and necessary benefits and blessings. Identity, purpose, vision, inheritance, and blessing all spring forth from this scriptural well. We always rejoice at the reception of these wonderful possessions but there is another side.

Immature ministers suffer opposition due to their own transgressions and lack of order. True men of God, however, always endure great opposition for the Word they carry and the dispensation of the gospel they have been called to complete.

When being in relationship with a true man of God, we can expect the reproaches that fall on him will also fall on us. In serving a ministry father, we will at times be required to carry his burden. True sons are not those willing to walk in fields of blessings. Rather they are those willing to walk the seldom-trodden path of association with true fathers who reap the opposition of the world and religion for the Word of God.

> *From that time many of His disciples went back, and walked no more with Him. Then said Jesus unto the twelve, Will ye also go away?*[7]
>
> *At my first answer no man stood with me, but all men forsook me.*[8]

There is no possibility of being a proper ministerial father to others unless you have first learned to become a true son. Due to the present condition and need of the Church at large, learning to be a son and rearing sons sometimes must occur concurrently. If we are not willing to be a son we have no right to become a father to others.

Religious systems have sometimes been so much out of order that in coming into this truth we may find we already have a number of ministers dependent upon us and under our authority. We can't just cut them loose to survive on their own until we obtain full stature as a father. We must, however, learn the lessons that only submission to a true father in ministry can teach.

Submission is a key word in understanding father/son order. God is not so much interested in the position we command in society or the great abilities of our gifting or even our deep understanding of the Scriptures. Much more than these He is interested in what kind of vessels we are for His use. Like willing clay in the hands of the potter, it is our submission more than any other characteristic that determines the character of our vessel.

True sons are those submitted to the father's voice, those who heed correction and follow direction. It is illegitimate sons (sons with no right to receive inheritance) who reject the counsel and rebuke of the father. Submission is not just obedience to a father but a willingness to not only heed the father's voice but also be about his business.

Jesus said, *"I must be about My Father's business."*[9] Unless the father's vision is in the forefront of our ministries, unless helping him achieve his purpose becomes the most important part of our focus, we are not truly submitted to a father. How can we as ministers expect godly submission from others if we are not in a position to give proper submission to a true father?

Qualification for Sonship

May be able to comprehend with all saints what is the breadth, and length, and depth, and height.[10]

Checking four areas of relationship with your spiritual father can test the qualification of your sonship. The four areas that qualify us for sonship are: being immersed in a father's vision and teaching; the ability to make the father's work your own; the willingness to submit to a father; and the desire to give honor. Maturity in these four areas brings maturity in relationship. By assessing these four areas of relationship we can gain an understanding of our level of relationship.

Width (work of father) +
Length (vision and teaching) +
Depth (submission) +
Height (honor) =
Submission as sons.

Width: Do I understand the necessity of being about the work of my father? Do I understand it must be my primary goal? Do I know how to do the work of my father?

Wist ye not that I must be about my Father's business?[11]

39

Length: Do I understand and advance the vision and teaching given my father from God? Do I understand that if it is given from God, it is not really his but the one's who gave it? Do I understand that if it is from God then I am following God but if it is only a man's vision then I am following a man and not God?

> *But thou hast fully known my doctrine, manner of life, purpose, faith, longsuffering, charity, patience.*[12]

> *Thou hast known the Holy Scriptures, which are able to make thee wise unto salvation.*[13]

Depth: Do I understand what biblical submission is? Do I understand how submitting to proper order is a submission to God? Do I know how to submit?

> *I beseech you, brethren...That ye submit yourselves unto such, and to every one that helpeth with us, and laboureth.*[14]

Height: Do I understand how honor shows the height of a son's relationship with his father? Do I know how to give honor to a father? Do I understand the difference between giving proper honor to a father and a counterfeit father who demands tribute?

> *Render therefore to all their dues: tribute to whom tribute is due; custom to whom custom; fear to whom fear; honor to whom honor.*[15]

> *Jesus prevented him, saying, What thinkest thou, Simon? of whom do the kings of the earth take custom or tribute? of their own children, or of strangers?*[16]

Assessing Our Own Maturity

Humble yourselves in the sight of the Lord, and He shall lift you up.[17]

Humble yourselves therefore under the mighty hand of God, that He may exalt you in due time.[18]

It is a somewhat paradoxical reality that only sons with maturity ever question their immaturity. True humility is a quality in precious supply within the Church. Yet if the ministry is to rise up into its rightful place at the proper time, God must be given opportunity to sift every thought and intent of the heart.

The ministry must allow the sometimes-painful process whereby every hope, plan, and desire within ministry is tested to see whether it is of God or man. True humility is the key to this process. Humility allows us to be strong in the Lord. Humility allows God to raise us to our rightful place in Him.

And whosoever shall exalt himself shall be abased; and he that shall humble himself shall be exalted.[19]

To become a proper father requires maturity and a willingness to endure adolescent behavior on the part of sons in the process of maturing. It is maturity that allows ministry to see afar off. Maturity sacrifices the promotion of self and the comfort of position for a posterity that will continue in the vision and purpose of God.

In ministry we must be willing to ask ourselves the hard questions. Do I have the maturity of a father? Is it possible I am only a boy leader? Am I willing to become what my sons need me to be? Am I a son in right order with my father? Am I motivated by those things that center on my ministry, gifting, or position or am I motivated out of a desire to fulfill purpose and give glory to the Father?

God already knows us. It is impossible to hide from Him. If we are to minister father/son order we need to let the Master Designer fashion His greatness out of our weaknesses, insecurities, and fears.

The Need to Have a Father's Heart

And he arose, and came to his father. But when he was yet a great way off, his father saw him, and had compassion, and ran, and fell on his neck, and kissed him.[20]

To be a proper ministry father, the Lord must give us a heart toward sons. One of the sad and disturbing sights of our day is the number of children being reared in households where fathers are unwilling to perform their dutiful role. If in the Spirit we assume the responsibility of becoming fathers, then it is incumbent upon us to put our children before any personal desires in our ministerial life.

We must be willing to provide for sons out of our spiritual possessions. Like the prodigal's father, our longing must be for the bringing of sons into right order. This man would not condone the actions of a wayward son, but his heart was always searching and waiting for both of his sons to enter right relationship.

Fathers with wrong hearts are always more interested in themselves than in their sons. They are willing to sacrifice the good of the son for personal benefit. Like Manasseh, they begin their rule as boys never maturing into true fathers.

And he made his son pass through the fire, and observed times, and used enchantments, and dealt with familiar spirits and wizards: he wrought much wickedness in the sight of the Lord, to provoke him to anger.[21]

It is of utmost importance for set ministry to establish father/son order in the church, to be a minister with a father's heart. Failure to do this will bring much pain to our ministries. David was a man of great spiritual insight and great prophetic gifting. He was chosen by God and elevated to the highest positions of authority. Years of struggle and suffering had tempered his spirit and molded his character.

He was a man of God. In the family order of the Bible even Jesus would be called the Son of David. Yet David as a parent failed his children in significant ways. For all his spiritual success, his failure to raise sons in order caused his greatest torment and the greatest threat to his kingdom. Incest, murder, and rebellion testify to his failure with his sons.

> And the king commanded Joab and Abishai and Ittai, saying, Deal gently for my sake with the young man, even with Absalom...And the king said unto Cushi, Is the young man Absalom safe? And Cushi answered, The enemies of my lord the king, and all that rise against thee to do thee hurt, be as that young man is. And the king was much moved, and went up to the chamber over the gate, and wept: and as he went, thus he said, O my son Absalom, my son, my son Absalom! Would God I had died for thee, O Absalom, my son, my son![22]

> Now Absalom in his lifetime had taken and reared up for himself a pillar, which is in the king's dale: for he said, I have no son to keep my name in remembrance.[23]

A wise ministry can learn from the example of David that ministerial accomplishment, great gifting, and even a strong relationship with the Lord are no substitute for the establishment of right order in sons. We can have spiritually endowed churches with tremendous outreach to our communities, churches that demonstrate great moves of God, that are still out of proper order and in danger of not being able to pass on inheritance.

David's failure to put his sons in order led directly to the rebellion of Absalom. His daughter was raped, his eldest son murdered, and now his son Absalom, who acted because his father was unwilling to act, was dead and much of Israel was ravished.

We can see in the story of Absalom a father who harbors regrets for failure to raise sons properly. We can see his great personal pain and longing for his son being pitted against his responsibilities to God and the nation. As he says *"My son, my son"* repeatedly, it is almost like he is trying to evoke a double annunciation of deity to erase his failure and undo the colossal events of the day.

David's son who tries to steal the inheritance winds up dead. David will never be able to pass on inheritance to him. Like all who do not follow proper order, Absalom resigns himself to having no son, no future, no generation: *"Absalom...reared up for himself a pillar, which is in the king's dale: for he said, I have no son to keep my name in remembrance."*[24]

His promise ceases upon his death. Unless the hearts of our ministries turn toward sons, we in our settings will witness, like David, the passing of sons with promise but no order. How much better in ministry to have one wife and bring forth one son of promise than to give birth to the disorder of a multitude of spiritual families with an abundance of confused descendants.

Even Solomon, *"the wisest man who ever lived,"* who inherits the kingdom from David, is incapable in all his wisdom of establishing proper order in his descendants. The kingdom will be divided in the days of his son; it will become a denomi*nation*. He is like his father and has too many wives.

Like ministers involved in too many intimate relationships that are able to give birth to conflicting aspects of ministry, so is David with his wives. One wife will give him a firstborn son of inheritance who is also a son of perversion. Another wife will give him a son of great beauty and charisma who is also a son of rebellion.

Still another wife will give him a son of wisdom who is also a son who will build an altar to Chemosh on which to sacrifice the sons of Israel.

Though David is three millenniums removed from us in time, yet his family disorder still speaks to us as ministers of God. This disorder warns and admonishes us that the power of our personal walk provides no guarantee of future generational order or a ministry that will carry on past our death. Even if, like David, we have the promise of a Messiah through our lineage, we and our descendants will have to pay a great price for not bringing our generations into order. We must not allow the importance of our positions and the opportunities of ministry to interfere with the proper rearing of sons.

Checklist on Preparation to Be Fathers

1. Do I have proper maturity?
2. Do I have ulterior motives?
3. Am I in right relationship with a spiritual father?
4. Is my heart to be a father?
5. What is my father's vision?
6. What is my vision?
7. What is the order of establishing sonship?
8. Am I willing to be changed and seek the preparation required for fatherhood?

ENDNOTES

1. Luke 1:17.
2. 2 Chronicles 29:35-36.
3. Matthew 20:25-28.
4. Mark 10:45.
5. Isaiah 58:7.
6. Romans 15:3.

7. John 6:66-67.
8. 2 Timothy 4:16.
9. Luke 2:49.
10. Ephesians 3:18.
11. Luke 2:49.
12. 2 Timothy 3:10.
13. 2 Timothy 3:15.
14. 1 Corinthians 16:15-16.
15. Romans 13:7.
16. Matthew 17:25.
17. James 4:10.
18. 1 Peter 5:6.
19. Matthew 23:12.
20. Luke 15:20.
21. 2 Kings 21:6.
22. 2 Samuel 18:5,32-33.
23. 2 Samuel 18:18.
24. 2 Samuel 18:18.

CHAPTER THREE

PREPARING THE PEOPLE TO RECEIVE

O Lord God of Abraham, Isaac, and of Israel, our fathers, keep this for ever in the imagination of the thoughts of the heart of Thy people, and prepare their heart unto Thee.[1]

And Hezekiah rejoiced, and all the people, that God had prepared the people: for the thing was done suddenly.[2]

*To turn the hearts of the fathers to the children... to make ready a **people prepared** for the Lord. So the service of the house of the Lord was set in order... God had **prepared the people**: for the thing was done suddenly.*[3]

*W*ithin the heart of every mature minister beats a God-given longing to see the completion of the work entrusted into his care. While some are overtaken in a quest for numbers or the Church's acknowledgment of their spiritual value, mature ministry empties itself in an effort to see the growth of Christ within the saints. This growth is seen as the ministry becomes replicated in those under the ministry's care. The passing on of perpetual inheritance is one of the greatest evidences of not only our faith but also the completion of our work.

As much as we may desire to witness growth and change within the saints, we as ministers realize we are powerless aside from God in bringing it to pass. A large part of our efforts often center on getting the saints to understand and walk in the vision and revelation of the Church. It often becomes glaringly apparent that much more is taught than is caught by our congregations. In establishing father/son order we have a biblical method to bring forth in our churches all the work entrusted into our care. Without preparation for father/son ministry this will never happen.

In almost every aspect of life we see that preparation must precede production. In the Church we should also be aware that instruction and preparation are not the same things. When we have given instruction, we have not necessarily prepared a son to walk in that instruction. Whether shaping a football team for victory, a business for expansion, a student for the workplace, or a church for ministry, the quality of preparation will determine the effectiveness of the product.

A professional football team, through drills, films, teaching, discipline, motivation, repetition, and rehearsal, will prepare 40-50 hours per week to play 60 minutes of football. In the world, success by and large is a consequence of effective preparation. In the Church, having the Spirit and teaching biblical truths are not substitutes for preparation but supernatural tools to bring forth a Church *"prepared unto every good work."*

The distance between a promise from God and the fulfillment of that promise is usually marked by our preparation. In our ministerial lives the Lord has given each of us varying promises for our lives and our individual ministries. These promises are usually conditional, requiring some response or change on our part.

The reason many Christians never see the completion of some promises made them is often due to the lack of preparation that is necessary to bring these promises to pass. Abraham was the inheritor of a new land. He was the father of nations, very rich and the friend of God, but these things required preparation. Abraham had to leave a familiar land, learn to trust God, and most of all allow God to change his thoughts.

All who minister in the Word of God have known what it is like to receive a revelation or understand a truth that could greatly change a person or congregation. All who minister, at times, have also seen the teaching of that truth or revelation received with superficial acceptance by those it was intended to help. We have come to understand that no matter how powerful the doctrine, no matter how right the intention, no matter how beneficial the teaching, and no matter how great the need on the part of the congregation, lack of preparation will cause severe limitation.

Unless the people are prepared, they will not be able to implement what is being taught. Unless the proper order is understood by the pastor, all his preaching will produce little action on the part of the saints. A congregation not prepared in how to walk in father/son order will always have difficulty in receiving and maturing.

The wise pastor has learned, however, that if the congregation is to walk in the Spirit, he must learn to minister as the Spirit ministers. The Spirit whispers and convicts; the enemy yells and condemns. The Spirit appeals to truth; the enemy to fear. The Spirit asks to be invited; the enemy demands to be listened to and obeyed. The Spirit invokes love, power, and a sound mind; the enemy fosters separation, self-righteousness, and confusion.

Though the Spirit is an easily entreated Spirit, He will not force His thoughts into a mind that has not been prepared to receive a "present" word. In John chapter 12 the voice of the Father came forth from Heaven. The Son heard the Father say that He has and would again glorify His name. Some who heard it said it thundered, others that an angel had spoken to Jesus, but only a Son could hear the clear and distinct word.

Saints not prepared as sons will have a hard time hearing the distinct Word from God regarding ministry. Good ministers have toiled year by year sharing good messages with good saints who have not been prepared to receive. In conveying father/son relationship to a congregation, it is imperative that the people have been prepared to receive this particular message. Good seed sowed into unprepared ground will produce little growth.

Preparation Requires the People to Desire Order

And Samuel spake unto all the house of Israel, saying, If ye do return unto the Lord with all your hearts, then put away the strange gods and Ashtaroth from among you, and prepare your hearts unto the Lord, and serve Him only: and He will deliver you out of the hand of the Philistines.[4]

Go through, go through the gates; prepare ye the way of the people; cast up, cast up the highway; gather out the stones; lift up a standard for the people.[5]

Many saints struggle with temptations and shortcomings. These muzzle their spirit man and imprison the divine light in their hearts within a wall of unyielding flesh dominated by self-desire. They are usually not at enmity with God nor insensitive to the Holy Spirit. They are, however, deficient in positioning their lives to allow the Spirit's control of all areas. *"For what I would, that do I not; but what I hate, that do I."*[6] It is not that most Christians do not know the answer to their needs; it is that they lack the spiritual order to make those answers a reality in their lives.

This is the condition of an anemic Church. The pastor is forever trying to put out fires, make people happy, and find solutions for every problem and answers for every need. It is not knowledge but order that frees a church to walk in ministry.

Think of the operation of the natural world. It is usually not the wisest, most dedicated and honest individual that rises to the height of political power. It is rarely the intellectuals or those with great knowledge who rise to rulership over nations but those, whether good or bad, who have *ordered* their lives to acquire and exercise power. They may be devoid of wisdom to govern in a godly manner. They may have little understanding of economics and even less concern for the welfare of the people, but if they have *ordered* their political lives in the area of power, they can rule for a lifetime.

In business, it is not the 4.0, Phi Beta Kappa, graduates from Ivy League business schools who dominate the boardrooms of American enterprise. Usually intelligent executives of the more common type fill these positions. Their distinguishing feature is that they are *ordered* in interpersonal skills such as communication, motivation, and relationship building and they know how to utilize existing corporate structure (order).

So in the Church it is not the mastery of the Bible or the demonstration of gifting, as important as these are, that determines the effective operation of ministry, but the *order* of the house. Is the local house of God ordered after father/son principles? Does the pastor understand this biblical order and is he able and willing to implement it?

Religion points to gifting as the central element of ministry. Many Christians are falsely taught that to find and walk in their gifting is their ministry. That is why we often hear of such things as healing ministry, counseling ministry, praise ministry, and the like. These may be giftings through which we minister, but the

Bible does not classify them as ministries. Our gifting determines how we minister, but it is not our ministry!

The church world by and large has saints seeking after gifting rather than order. Gifting tends to focus on *me*; order focuses on relationship and the *Body*. The set minister, in establishing father/son principles, must help saints understand and desire order and the fulfillment of the vision of the Body above personal accomplishment.

This of course works against innate human desires to achieve position and gain notoriety. If our congregations can be shown the value of order in their personal as well as their corporate lives, they will follow. The direction, purpose, identity, and ministry offered by father/son relationships is a missing piece of their spiritual lives that many are looking for.

Teaching the People to Suffer Successfully
(Learning to Love the Process and Not Just the Reward)

Though He were a Son, yet learned He obedience by the things which He suffered.[7]

As many as desire to make a fair show in the flesh, they constrain you to be circumcised; only lest they should suffer persecution for the cross of Christ.[8]

In modern Christianity, as in modern life, there is little under-standing of the place for suffering. Some are taught that the proper exercise of faith negates all suffering. Trials that the Lord allows for our sanctification and perfection are often denounced as attacks from the enemy. In pseudo-Christianity, saints are taught to curse their wildernesses—the very place from which God will bring forth their purpose and ministry.

Successful suffering teaches us discipline that leads to order. Disciplining our children may cause them mild suffering, but the intended end of that suffering is an ordered life in which the desires of the flesh are kept in check. Children who are improperly punished or who receive no godly correction to their flesh grow up selfish, irresponsible, and unruly. They are unable to submit the desires of the flesh to the higher purpose of the Spirit—untrained in righteousness. So it is in any church where the people have not been taught to suffer successfully.

Suffering is that process whereby the Lord deals with the weakness of the flesh so that we can be vessels *"prepared unto every good work."*[9] It is not the set minister's purpose to bring suffering to the Church, but it should be his purpose to teach the people to discern trials allowed by the Lord and how to permit those trials to mold their spiritual character.

> *And not only so, but we glory in tribulations also: knowing that tribulation worketh patience; and patience, experience and experience hope.*[10]

Why do so many Christians live in hopelessness? Because their character has not been fully formed. Why has their character not been fully formed? Because they lack patience or endurance. Why do they lack endurance? Because they have not been taught how to successfully handle the suffering from tribulation. You see it's an *order*. Suffering successfully builds in us endurance. Endurance builds in us character, which is the godly handling of all life experiences; and character in us produces a hope based on God's truth and not on worldly circumstances.

Jesus was a son who learned obedience by the things He suffered. We and our ministry sons will learn the same way. A church that has not been taught to suffer successfully will never follow father/son order.

> *Yea, and all that will live godly in Christ Jesus shall suffer persecution.*[11]

If we suffer, we shall also reign with Him.[12]

And if children, then heirs; heirs of God, and joint-heirs with Christ; if so be that we suffer with Him, that we may be also glorified together.[13]

For unto you it is given in the behalf of Christ, not only to believe on Him, but also to suffer for His sake.[14]

That ye may be counted worthy of the kingdom of God, for which ye also suffer.[15]

Choosing rather to suffer affliction with the people of God, than to enjoy the pleasures of sin for a season.[16]

Wherefore let them that suffer according to the will of God commit the keeping of their souls to Him in well doing, as unto a faithful Creator.[17]

We need to learn and to teach our congregations how to love the process and not just the reward. "*My brethren, count it all joy when ye fall into divers temptations.*"[18] The joy in God is not just found in attaining a spiritual goal or blessing but in the daily life-transforming process leading to our perfection. Learning to walk in father/son order must be formed out of a joy and not of necessity or obligation.

Teaching the Specifics of Father/Son Order

*And with many such parables spake He the word unto them, as they were **able to hear** it.*[19]

Ability to hear the father/son message is dependent on maturity and desire. Simply teaching the principles of this order and expecting the church to follow it is not spiritually realistic.

Father/son order is a process of relationship and not just a teaching. General instruction should be given by the set ministry to the entire church, but specific training should be given to each son individually and, at times, to sons in a general gathering by their specific father. It is the only way this teaching can become relational. It must become a relationship and not just an organizational tool.

Not all in our churches are ready to come into father/son order. As with a natural family, there are those who are too young or self-absorbed to even understand who or what a father is. Others are too immature to follow. For these, general teaching to the church is important.

There is no useful purpose in trying to bring the young or immature into father/son order before they approach spiritual adulthood. These should be encouraged to pray and seek God in this area and to be confident that in the proper time He will bring forth their ministry father. *They don't have to make it happen.* Relationships have to be built in maturity and tested by time.

The People Need to Understand Generational Order

Within our local churches there is need to establish a generational order. Not all in church are the set minister's direct sons. In a healthy church there should be many fathers ordered in their generations. In fact, one of the problems in Corinth was that they did not have enough fathers in order.

> *For though ye have ten thousand instructors in Christ, yet have ye not many fathers: for in Christ Jesus I have begotten you through the gospel.*[20]

In father/son order we each have only one direct ministry father and a few others who are fathers to us through the order of the generations—ministry grandfathers and great grandfathers.

Though this Scripture is speaking more directly to that issue, we can also understand it in the general need of the Church to follow fathers and not the immature in ministry. There was a multitude of boy instructors in Corinth because there were not enough fathers in order. They had some, but their generations were not ordered. (This area is covered in detail in a later section.)

Responsibility to Train Up Sons

Only set ministry can call forth sons in their proper generations.

We need to allow the Spirit to distinguish between those who are legitimate sons and those who are illegitimate, to distinguish between the mature and the immature, and those of the second generation from those of other generations. If we are going to call forth sons, then we have the absolute responsibility to see that they are trained.

If we are unwilling or unprepared to train up sons, we have no right to call them forth. It would be far better not to call a son than to call him forth into relationship and allow him to live in continual adolescence because of our lack of preparation or willingness, on our part, to bring direction and relationship into his life. Anyone who in the natural sires a child has certain responsibilities toward that child; so it is in father/son ministry.

Preparing for Father/Son Order Requires
Repetition and Consistency in Teaching

All of us who truly understand the significance of father/son order aspire to have this order function fully in our churches. We understand the growth that such order will bring to the church. We anticipate the completion of our God-given vision that can only come through such a pattern. We recognize its necessity in bringing forth our full measure of rule.

People do not generally follow merely because they hear a spiritual teaching. They follow the teaching because it brings an experience to them, an avenue to connect with God. Any teaching, including father/son, has to affect them personally before we can expect its implementation.

As significant as father/son order is, it is only one of many biblical truths that form lines of connection with our heavenly Father. It takes time and repetition to teach it to our churches. Hearing about this teaching a few times will not bring any church into this order. More than just sharing teachings, the set ministry has to build relationship to make this order successful.

When bringing this instruction to the church, the saint who does not grasp what the set ministry is trying to accomplish may wonder if the Bible contains any other teaching. This is because it requires much time and emphasis to be placed upon acquiring this relationship. Jesus taught in lines of understanding to His disciples and taught with much repetition. The words of the most important man to ever walk the earth are mostly contained in a few thousand words scattered throughout four short books.

When you study the Gospels you see that Jesus spoke many things over and over and numerous teachings of Jesus are repeated several times in these books. In part, it is an illustration of how doctrine must not only be taught but discipled in the Church. Since the Holy Spirit did not consider it a waste of Bible space to repeat events and teachings of Jesus, we should learn that there is a method to teaching believers to follow.

Father/son order is only one line of doctrine within the Word, but it is a line upon which so many other teachings depend for their fulfillment. The foundation of a house is an inconspicuous and mostly hidden part of the structure. Yet all other parts rest upon the strength and integrity of its substructure to define their order and intended purpose; so it is within the Church. The building of father/son relationships within the Church provides the foundation and order upon which most other doctrines depend. Once it is established, emphasis on father/son teaching can greatly diminish as other doctrines are built upon its foundation.

Establishing the Church in Truth

There is an obvious need to see that our churches are following biblical truth—especially as through growth we come to increasingly understand what that means. Unless the end result of our efforts is the promotion and reception of truth, we will never comprehend in His fullness Jesus, who is the Truth.

Areas of doctrine on which relationships are based are most important to father/son order. Are marriages and families in order or are they patterned after the world more than the Word? Are the people in church truly brothers and sisters or are they disconnected members that happen to meet together once or twice a week? One of the areas that defines willingness for relationship in church is the issue of tithing.

Tithing not only defines the willingness of the people, but also the willingness of ministry. Unfortunately in many religious settings, tithing has become the preeminent doctrine of the Church. What should be a doctrine of great purpose and connection has often become a doctrine of separation. Pastors demand tithe, but it is often more out of a desire for, or a perceived right to, income than a desire for the welfare of the saints.

In their appeals for tithe, some use manipulation and fear to motivate the people to part with their money. Saints grudgingly or blindly give without any more understanding than that the Bible says to do it, or that in giving they can become materially prosperous. Instead of linking the people of God, the misapplication of this teaching has in many cases divided the people, each seeking their own good and not that of the Body.

If anything, biblical tithing should speak of relationship and generation. To establish proper father/son order, ministries as well as saints need to understand and practice biblical tithing. The priesthood needs to establish proper tithing order in their ministries so the people can receive the spiritual reward of their obedience.

One aspect of this is the understanding of the "power of the tithe," to connect us in order through Abraham. Levi, the fourth generation of Abraham's family, was connected through the tithe. This has great significance to the order of the Church.

And as I may so say, Levi also, who receiveth tithes, payed tithes in Abraham.[21]

This was a charge that predated the law and was instituted by Abraham in paying tithe to Melchizedek, which linked him all the way back to Adam. In other words, it connected him in the generations. Now there are a number of reasons why this is important in bringing forth the family of God. Ministers and saints need to be prepared to tithe properly. Ministers as well as saints need to tithe. That tithe is not to an organization or to a church but through ordered generations. If we are unwilling to come into father/son order, then the issue of tithing is really of secondary importance.

God uses natural acts of obedience on earth to connect us to heavenly blessing and purpose. Marriage, worship, clothing, tithing, human government, and other foundations all have their beginnings in the Book of Genesis. Each requires a natural act to make a heavenly connection. Failure to perform what God requires in the natural negates order in the spiritual.

Many, especially today, feel that the act of marriage is passé—a holdover from previous days when society was less enlightened. "What really counts is that you truly care for one another; not whether you've participated in a ceremony of marriage." Human reasoning can try to negate the Word but not without consequences. Without a pronouncement of union before God and man, the blessings that should come forth from that union will be negated. To receive the heavenly blessing requires the natural act.

The natural act is a point of obedience connecting what is accomplished in Heaven and bringing it to pass in the earth. This is true in every area and especially in establishing father/son order. Perverting the tithe by making saints feel as though they will be cursed by God with financial poverty unless they give works contrary to God's order. The tithe, to those who apply it righteously, carries with it the promise of connection in the generations through Abraham all the way back to the original seed.

Possible Unintended Consequences of Teaching Father/Son Order

We should be aware of some unintended consequences of teaching this order to our churches. To anything of value there is a price. If we fail to teach father/son order to our churches or teach it improperly, we lock up the future potential of the generations that would come forth from their spiritual loins. There are some who will improperly use this teaching to elevate their personal ministries rather than establish biblical order within the church. Depending on the local church's history and organization, this teaching can cause great adjustments.

Leadership reared and trained in denominational structures may find great difficulty in adjusting to ministry dominated by father/son relationship. Spirits that are in opposition—and there always are some from the least likely places—will manifest and have to be dealt with. Not everyone will think it is a good idea.

Some may fear for a loss of position, some may think it is following man and not God. Whatever the scenario, there is usually opposition that may even involve the temporary loss of church membership. It may also give opportunity to those in religion to criticize your ministry. If done by the Spirit, however, it will bring an order that will make the completion of the Church's purpose possible. A prepared Church is an empowered Church.

ENDNOTES

1. 1 Chronicles 29:18.
2. 2 Chronicles 29:36.
3. 2 Chronicles 29:35b, 36b.
4. 1 Samuel 7:3.
5. Isaiah 62:10.
6. Romans 7:15.
7. Hebrews 5:8.
8. Galatians 6:12.
9. 2 Timothy 2:21.
10. Romans 5:3-4.
11. 2 Timothy 3:12.
12. 2 Timothy 2:12.
13. Romans 8:17.
14. Philippians 1:29.
15. 2 Thessalonians 1:5.
16. Hebrews 11:25.
17. 1 Peter 4:19.
18. James 1:2.
19. Mark 4:33.
20. 1 Corinthians 4:15.
21. Hebrews 7:9.

Chapter Four

Proper Vision Is Central to Building Proper Order

*I*n *the Church world* today much is said about vision. Like all Bible terms, our definition influences our understanding. An improper definition will lead to an improper or incomplete understanding. The Bible is written using comparison, allegories, and definition. As with the phrase "baptism of the Holy Spirit," the definition as to what the baptism of the Holy Spirit is greatly influences what a particular pastor or church is willing to understand and believe about the operation of the Holy Spirit.

Vision is simply the ability to see. In Scripture, it is the ability to see, according to God's choosing, what God has done in the heavens so that it may be accomplished on earth. It is impossible to properly lead people without a well-defined vision. Vision sets a mark in the Spirit toward which the people can work. If it is missing or confused, then the people have no ability to adequately define their ministries or to receive a proper vision of their own. Disunity of the Body and lack of positive direction are the consequence.

What is commonly called vision in the Church today is often little more than a business plan by church leaders for the promotion of their ministries and churches. Even visions that come from the mind of man can produce worldly success (numbers, money, notoriety) within the church. These types of visions usually speak of the call of God on a leader to win a city or a country or even the entire world for Christ.

A vision from God in which the church can find biblical order is something quite different from these. To lead requires vision. It is the obligation of all leadership to provide vision. *"Where there is no vision, the people perish."*[1] That is to say, they cast off restraint; there is no vision to keep them focused or to give them understanding of what the Lord is doing in their local setting. The vision God calls leadership to is the vision of His purpose contained in the heavens.

Prepared to Receive Vision

And Moses said, I will now turn aside, and see this great sight, why the bush is not burnt. And when the Lord saw that he turned aside to see, God called unto him out of the midst of the bush, and said, Moses, Moses. And he said, Here am I.[2]

God was getting Moses' attention by doing something supernatural with the natural world. Moses had to turn aside to see what the burning bush was all about. To gain vision we have to be willing to turn aside from our normal, ingrained routine—to be willing to stop doing all those good things the Lord never told us to do.

This will usually require a supernatural intervention by fire—not a fire of destruction but fire of construction in your life. It was only when the Lord saw that Moses turned that He spoke to him out of the fire His vision for Moses (the set man) and Israel. The ability to see the supernatural is not enough; we have to be willing to turn aside to hear God's voice of vision through the supernatural.

Moses was a leader. Like all leaders he needed preparation. He would have been unwilling naturally to gain this preparation, seeing he was in a position to partake of the riches and fruits of Egypt. After all, he was educated in the best schools of Egypt, knew the most influential men of the land, and was trained in being part of the ruling class. What other preparation could he need?

As with us, the Lord had to allow some unpleasant circumstances to move Moses into hidden places to be instructed in a wilderness. His 40-year time of preparation was coming to an end. He needed a vision from Heaven—a vision that would give him the understanding, direction, and confidence to lead God's people—a vision not of himself or born out of his desires for the people, but a vision that would speak from God to the people, a vision upon which all willing hearts in Israel could build.

God spoke to Moses saying, "*Moses, Moses*," using his name in a double enunciation. This double pronouncement confirmed that God Himself would establish His heavenly purpose for Israel in the earth through Moses. Godly vision always involves seeing in the heavens and being confirmed that He will establish it here on earth.

Vision and Purpose Are Always Expanding

And I am come down to deliver them out of the hand of the Egyptians, and to bring them up out of that land unto a good land and a large, unto a land flowing with milk and honey.[3]

In Exodus chapters 3 and 4, God speaks vision and purpose to Moses. Our understanding of our vision and purpose in God is always expanding. We do not get the whole loaf at one time, but vision and purpose are parceled out as we grow in the Lord.

Come now therefore, and I will send thee unto Pharaoh, that thou mayest bring forth My people the children of Israel out of Egypt.[4]

With this one statement, God summarized for Moses his purpose for which he had been waiting 80 years. It was not Moses' complete purpose but an outline to which many other parts would be added. His vision for Moses' ministry and that of Israel is interspersed throughout these chapters, specific elements of which are spoken of many times by other Bible writers.

God planned to move Israel—He was listening. He would visit them and would also speak through Moses to the children of Israel and to Pharaoh. He planned to take away their bondage, answer their cry, and empower Moses as His instrument to accomplish this. God would reveal His name (nature) to them. He would lead them to a land of promise.

What a vision! It wasn't the complete vision—more would come at Sinai and other places—but it gave the people direction, understanding, purpose, and a vision into which others, if spiritual like Joshua, could receive their specific vision. Our vision for our churches should incorporate similar characteristics.

The Place of Vision

Now Moses kept the flock of Jethro his father in law, the priest of Midian: and he led the flock to the backside of the desert, and came to the mountain of God, even to Horeb.[5]

Notice where Moses was and what he was doing when this light of vision and purpose pierced his life. He was in the desert near Horeb (waste) tending the flock of Jethro (excellence), his *father*-in-law. He was not dwelling in the cities where the daily exchange of goods and interaction of the masses occur. He was not doing some illustrious work to which others took notice. He was not in the spotlight of man's adoration or in a position of power that he had once held. He was in a desert place tending another's sheep.

What are the usual circumstances in which vision and purpose are found in our lives? It will be in deserted places where we are empty of an atmosphere of self-promotion and the confusion and opinion of religious thinking. It will be while we are tending the flock (saints) and doing the "present" work the Lord has given into our hand. It will be while we are doing the work of our father in ministry and following the excellence of that relationship.

While so engaged, the Lord brings us to our own Horeb. The world may think of it as a waste of time, but it is really the mountain of God—waste or empty of everything but God Himself! In this manner, the Lord brings vision and from such surroundings He brings forth purpose. It is always in the mountain (the highest point of spiritual revelation) where the view of Heaven is the clearest.

Promises of God Versus Vision From God

If we look at most visions recorded in the Scripture, we see that they involve instructions related to a journey. Abraham, Moses, Noah, Daniel, Ezekiel, Paul, and John all had visions that spoke of journeying to new lands or higher places in the land. Set ministry needs to expect that vision for ministry or a church will involve direction in journeys that will lead to higher realms in God. If we are not seeing in the heavens what should be completed here on earth, we have to question whether it is really a vision from God or merely our own sincere desire for the Lord to act in our ministry or church.

Many visions can be nothing more than a wish list in which ministries hope to gain God's participation and the people's acceptance by calling it a "vision" from the Lord. "God is going to give us a large and well-appointed, new church building"; or "The Lord is going to use this church to win this city for Christ"; or "The Lord is going to prosper us beyond our wildest dreams and show the lost that He owns the riches of the world." These are all nice sentiments, but if true they speak more of promises than they do of vision from the Lord. Promises from God are by themselves not vision.

True Vision Will Be Part of Our Ministry Father's Vision

Most visions that come from religion speak of God's changing our natural circumstances. They are almost devoid of direction or heavenly purpose or any understanding of reaching higher in God. A true vision from the Lord will be part of another vision. If I don't know my father's vision, I will never be able to fully receive God's vision for my ministry.

If I can't write down and explain the vision of my ministry father, how will I ever pass the elements of that vision on to my sons? If I don't understand my father's vision, how will I fully grasp the vision the Lord would give me? I won't; it's impossible. Unless vision grows and progresses through the generations, the purpose of God in our lives will never fully develop.

As we mature, the Lord speaks vision into our ministries. My vision, although not identical, must be related to and come forth from my father's vision. If this does not happen, there will be two opposing visions in the ministry family causing division. Di*vision*, in this sense, literally means two visions or the separation of vision.

This is why people who do not agree with or promote the vision of the house will always cause division and a lack of unity. They don't see it as their vision or the vision of God for the house, but a man's vision. A true vision for a ministry will always provide direction and opportunity for all under that vision to receive a distinct personal vision that can be integrated into the larger vision.

Godly vision, not gifting or doctrine, is the foundation upon which the unity of the Body is bound together by love. God has a general vision: to save the lost and restore the world unto Himself. This is spoken of in the Gospel references as the Great Commission.

The way He brings the Great Commission to pass is to give "set ministries" specific portions of that general vision.

These in turn are broken down further to those under the set ministries' vision—the principle of father to son. In so doing, the complete vision of God is accomplished and the entire Body is connected through a commonality of vision in the unity of faith. The problem, of course, is that the Church by and large is not operating under father/son order nor seeking this type of vision.

Ministry Is Built on Vision and Is Progressive

And when we were all fallen to the earth, I heard a voice speaking unto me, and saying in the Hebrew tongue, Saul, Saul, why persecutest thou Me? It is hard for thee to kick against the pricks. And I said, Who art Thou, Lord? And He said, I am Jesus whom thou persecutest. But rise, and stand upon thy feet: for I have appeared unto thee for this purpose, to make thee a minister and a witness both of these things which thou hast seen, and of those things in the which I will appear unto thee; delivering thee from the people, and from the Gentiles, unto whom now I send thee, to open their eyes, and to turn them from darkness to light, and from the power of Satan unto God, that they may receive forgiveness of sins, and inheritance among them which are sanctified by faith that is in Me. Whereupon, O king Agrippa, I was not disobedient unto the heavenly **vision**.[6]

The apostle Paul had need of a vision to complete the work of the Lord. His vision was not one of building buildings nor was it a promise that he would have thousands of followers. In fact, nowhere in his writings does he number the people of any of the churches he established. Later religious writers often romanticize his ministry, but it is probable that most people of the Roman

Empire outside of Christianity knew very little if anything of this messenger from God. Even a minor television preacher of today is probably recognized by more people than those who knew Paul in his entire lifetime.

His was a ministry that operated on scant resources. Much of his time was spent imprisoned inside cold stone walls with a stench reminiscent of an unkempt barnyard. At other times he labored with his hands to provide for the basic essentials of life—always in danger, continually being met with opposition.

He is often called great. Is this because of his writings we now cherish so dearly, or the great number of people he influenced, or is it due to the immense spiritual power and miracles that emanated from his ministry? Perhaps it is a combination of all these, yet he saw his ministry in direct contradiction to the fame we now so abundantly lavish on him today. He was not blinded in his heavenly purpose by the worldly pull of fame, power, or financial prosperity.

Paul's greatness is obvious to those who aspire to heavenly manifestation. It lays in the fact that he was on a quest to know Jesus. His was not just an association but a relationship with the Creator. Beyond this he knew what so many in Christianity never acquire. He had a vision from God and knew his identity and his purpose independent of man or organization.

He knew when his ministry was completed: "I have finished my course." The reason he knew this was because he had a vision and understood his purpose. Paul knew what he was supposed to accomplish and when it was completed. Too often ministries fail to turn at a spiritual intersection or follow a new artery of ministry because they do not have clear vision.

Many think their ministries should go on in perpetuity, building, growing, and flourishing. They have no idea when their ministry should veer or markedly be altered because they have not clearly seen their vision. Paul finished the portion of the vision of

God allotted into his care. That portion is complete, but our portions are still in the process of being fulfilled if we have proper vision and know our purpose.

The apostle Paul's vision, as all visions, was progressive. In Acts chapters 9, 22, and 26, we have recorded three listings of the same episode. In each of the three we see information related to the vision he received from the Lord. In each subsequent retelling of the event, Paul gives greater detail of those things pertaining to his vision. As he walked in ministry, the vision became clearer and clearer. Areas he did not fully understand became more distinct as natural events confirmed the spiritual pronouncements of the vision.

> *Whereupon, O king Agrippa, I was not disobedient unto the heavenly vision.*[7]

Paul's conclusion before King Agrippa of his ministry was that he was not disobedient to the vision. Completion of our ministries likewise is conditioned upon our obedience in understanding and fulfilling our vision.

Vision Must Be Received, Written, and Plain

> *I will stand upon my watch, and set me upon the tower, and will watch to see what He will say unto me, and what I shall answer when I am reproved. And the Lord answered me, and said, Write the vision, and make it plain upon tables, that he may run that readeth it. For the vision is yet for an appointed time, but at the end it shall speak, and not lie: though it tarry, wait for it; because it will surely come, it will not tarry.*[8]

The prophet is meditating on what the Lord would speak and how he would answer. As a prophet he stood watch over the land

and was set by God. The set ministry in a church incorporates this same function. God sets him over the work. He watches for the Lord to inquire before His presence. When God answers Habakkuk, He gives him a vision.

The Lord tells Habakkuk to write the vision. A vision that is not written will always be unclear; it will be left open to personal interpretation. Writing our visions will do at least three things for us that cannot be accomplished in any other way.

1. First, it will clarify and refine the vision in our minds, allowing God to add understanding and insight to us.
2. Second, it will give the people a concrete outline in understanding the purpose and direction of the church and their personal ministries and visions.
3. Third, it allows our vision to be carried on in subsequent generations.

The Lord tells Habakkuk to make the vision *plain*. Is our vision understandable? Is it easy for others to see what is to be done and how it is connected to our father's vision? It has to be plain so *"that he may run that readeth it."* How can our visions be read unless they are written?

How can our sons and churches follow, unless we make it plain? Clear vision will allow the church to be unified in direction, ministry, and purpose.

There is a simple test you can do to check whether or not your vision is understood and will become perpetual throughout your house. Have your sons write down your vision on one side of a piece of paper. If they cannot, your vision will never be implemented in the church. How can they pass on that which they do not know or understand? If they write varying accounts of your vision, leaving out significant parts or adding things that should not be there, then perhaps you have not clearly implemented the vision in your house in a way that can be understood and followed.

Can we as set ministry write down our vision from the Lord for our ministry and church? If not, how are our sons and our churches supposed to implement what we cannot explain? If you have no written vision, how will your sons be able to fit their vision from the Lord into yours?

Finally, a written and plain vision gives our sons and the church hope, direction, confidence, and faith. *"For the vision is yet for an appointed time, but at the end it shall speak, and not lie: though it tarry, wait for it; because it will surely come, it will not tarry."*[9]

The people will have confidence in what they are doing and will not be carried away by various doctrines or world events, because they know what God is doing and what their purpose is in the vision He's given. They can live in patience because they understand what God is bringing to pass.

Receiving a Vision From the Lord

Thus saith the Lord of hosts, Hearken not unto the words of the prophets that prophesy unto you: they make you vain: they speak a vision of their own heart, and not out of the mouth of the Lord.[10]

And the child Samuel ministered unto the Lord before Eli. And the word of the Lord was precious in those days; there was no open vision.[11]

Are all visions true? Obviously not. How then can we acquire godly vision and distinguish between that which is of man and that which is from God? In some ways our day is like that of the time of Eli; the priesthood is defiled, the spiritual order of father and son is fractured, the church is relying on past experience and signs from God. Patriarchs of a message understand that their ministries in some ways, like that of Samuel's, are transitional, leading to the reestablishment of father/son order.

> *Her gates are sunk into the ground; he hath destroyed*
> *and broken her bars: her king and her princes are*
> *among the Gentiles: the law is no more; her prophets*
> *also find no vision from the Lord.*[12]

Because the church world is so out of order, its gates are sunk (no access to proper authority), its bars are broken (no divine protection), and there is no vision from the Lord. The vision that comes forth, by and large, is a vision spoken out of the heart and not from a visitation of the Lord. This is why these visions usually speak only of promises and great exploits.

> *And some of the Pharisees which were with Him heard*
> *these words, and said unto Him, Are we blind also? Jesus*
> *said unto them, If ye were blind, ye should have no sin:*
> *but now ye say, We see; therefore your sin remaineth.*[13]

The parables and instances of healing the blind in the Gospels are spiritual examples for us about godly vision or the lack thereof. To be blind is the opposite of having vision. Jesus said that the consequence of being spiritually blind is that those who lead and those who follow would "*both fall into the ditch.*"[14]

They have no direction; they don't know where they are going; and they have no VISION! In Matthew chapter 23, Jesus pronounces woes upon religious leaders. Five times He calls them blind. They were blinded by money, by making constants variables and variables constants, and by only being able to judge by outward appearance. How could they receive vision from the Lord?

From the Gospels we learn that vision can be partial or perfect, that surrounding circumstances can influence vision, and that vision can be corrected or improved. Now these Gospel occurrences are certainly speaking of the personal condition of the heart, but in a broader sense they can be understood in ways that affect our ministries and churches.

John devotes the entire ninth chapter of his Gospel to the blind man, a type of ministry, and the effect his regaining sight had on the religious leaders. Jesus has come to bring sight to ministry. Those in religion, who think they see, will never see, being blinded by false judgment and self-righteousness. We need Jesus to anoint our eyes with vision to see into the Spirit's purpose in and through our ministries.

Visitation, preparation, relationship, prayer, father/son order, scriptural foundation, and hidden places are all terms related to finding God's vision for our ministries. As written earlier, those who receive godly vision usually receive it in a *hidden* place. Vision in the Bible invariably involves the *visitation* of the Lord. We are *prepared* by the Lord to be open to receive. It is birthed through *prayer* and our *relationship* with the Lord. It requires proper *order* in our lives. It is based on the *Word*.

Before the Lord ever explains His vision for us in natural terms, He usually gives us a Scripture or portion of Scripture. This word may burn in our hearts for a long period of time, through which He says to us in clear and unmistakable terms, "THIS IS YOU." Walking in father/son order requires clearer, higher, and truer vision than we have ever had before.

ENDNOTES

1. Proverbs 29:18.
2. Exodus 3:3-4.
3. Exodus 3:8.
4. Exodus 3:10.
5. Exodus 3:1.
6. Acts 26:14-19.

7. Acts 26:19.
8. Habakkuk 2:1-3.
9. Habakkuk 2:3.
10. Jeremiah 23:16.
11. 1 Samuel 3:1.
12. Lamentations 2:9.
13. John 9:40-41.
14. Luke 6:39.

CHAPTER FIVE

ESTABLISHING
GENERATIONAL ORDER

When the Lord shall build up Zion, He shall appear in His glory.[1]

*T*he *appearing* of the Lord is tied to the building up of Zion. From the remnant Church that the Lord is working with to bring His completed purpose shall come the perfection Zion. One of the understandings of the Hebrew word "build" (*banah*) is to obtain children. Is it possible that the method the Lord is using to build up Zion is the obtaining of children, or the establishing of generations? The Bible is a book of generations—the family of God traced through a spiritual lineage. It is written for the generations.

This shall be written for the generation to come: and the people which shall be created shall praise the Lord.[2]

The Need to Establish Generations for Ministry

These sought their register among those that were reckoned by genealogy, but they were not found: therefore were they, as polluted, put from the priesthood.[3]

THE ORDER OF A *Son*

In the Old Testament, a history of generations was necessary for ministry in the priesthood. Yet few, if any, in ministry today can trace their spiritual heritage through the generations. Some can cite a pastor or church organization or Christian ministry that was significant in their Christian walk or with which their family associated over time. Many may be able to say "my family has been part of this or that church or religion for so many years"—seeking identity or right to ministry by association with a church system. But who can go back through the generations and list their ancestral father-to-son connections and the spiritual inheritance that each of these connections passed on?

God has a method to reconnect His Church in its proper generations. To those who see the necessity of the father/son order in restoring wholeness in ministry and the fulfillment of the purpose of God, the Lord in this day is bringing forth the reestablishment of spiritual generations.

Instead of being subject to live in single portions with most of the spiritual inheritance being buried in the graves of previous generations, the Lord in this day will bring forth the continuing and increasing blessing of double portions. Only in making our ministries generational are we assured of a continuance and completion of the vision given us by the Lord.

> *He was taken from prison and from judgment: and who shall declare His generation? for He was cut off out of the land of the living: for the transgression of My people was He stricken.*[4]

> *A seed shall serve him; it shall be accounted to the Lord for a generation.*[5]

> *So all the generations from Abraham to David are fourteen generations; and from David until the carrying away into Babylon are fourteen generations; and from*

the carrying away into Babylon unto Christ are fourteen generations.[6]

Isaiah asks the question, "Who will declare the generation of Jesus?" He was stricken for the transgression of the people and cut off, leaving no natural children to carry on His generations. Yet the Scripture speaks of His offspring in numerous places. To this remnant, the offspring of the Lord, is reserved an order and a purpose which will bring forth the appearing of Christ. Jesus the head will be manifested to the world through His Body.

Matthew in his Gospel is careful to record the generations of Jesus, making note that there are three sets of 14 generations each. For Jesus' right to minister as the Son of Abraham and the Son of David, He would have to show a generational connection. He could not be their son unless He was connected.

When we carefully count each set we recognize that Jesus is listed as the thirteenth generation in the third set. It is stated that, *"from the carrying away into Babylon unto Christ are fourteen generations."* If Jesus is the thirteenth, then who is the Christ that is listed as the fourteenth generation? Is it possible it is not Jesus but His son? In Revelations 21:7, Jesus tells us that all who overcome are His son.

> *But every man in his own order: Christ the firstfruits; afterward they that are Christ's at His coming.*[7]

> *And they that are **Christ's** have crucified the flesh with the affections and lusts.*[8]

> *For the earnest expectation of the creature waiteth for the manifestation of the sons of God.*[9]

Following order, after Jesus' first appearing must come His manifestation in His son. The process of the revealing of this

THE ORDER OF A Son

man-child son will come through complete victory over the carnal mind by being transformed into the image of Christ. Jesus will appear in His generation.

The point of this is that God is bringing forth a righteous generation in our day. We need to understand that our purpose is not to occupy till He comes—holding on in the face of the storm, waiting for an escape. If we understand that we are to be the generation of Jesus, then we will seek the establishment of generational order in our churches. The seed that shall serve the Lord shall be accounted for His generation.

Biblical Patterns of Generational Order

Ye are the children of the prophets, and of the covenant which God made with our fathers, saying unto Abraham, And in thy seed shall all the kindreds of the earth be blessed.[10]

As He spake to our fathers, to Abraham, and to his seed for ever.[11]

There is a spiritual link in proper tithing that reconnects us with the promises of God made through Abraham. There is a blessing in tithing that is not usually presented to the Church world that does not properly understand and practice biblical tithing. The study of Abraham and his descendants also gives us a pattern of the importance of establishing generational order within our ministries.

As mentioned in Chapter Three, Abraham had received great promises from the Lord. He would become the father of many nations and the progenitor of innumerable descendants. So great were the promises and faith of this man, that God through our faith in Christ makes Abraham our ancestor.

And if ye be Christ's, then are ye Abraham's seed, and heirs according to the promise.[12]

Abraham had only one son of promise. He was dependent on Isaac not only to be in a position to receive inheritance, but also to be able to pass it on to other generations. God could promise Abraham a great name and lineage but only sons in generational order would have the ability to bring those promises to pass. The reason God could make such promises to Abraham was that in faith he was able to *"command his children and his household after him."*[13] God knew, "If I give these promises to Abraham, he will make sure to put his sons and household in order so that the promises will become continuous." The promises of God in our ministries are not dependent on our gifting or abilities, but they are dependent on our willingness to put our ministries and churches in order.

Moreover He said, I am the God of thy father, the God of Abraham, the God of Isaac, and the God of Jacob. And Moses hid his face; for he was afraid to look upon God.[14]

And the Lord was gracious unto them, and had compassion on them, and had respect unto them, because of His covenant with Abraham, Isaac, and Jacob, and would not destroy them, neither cast He them from His presence as yet.[15]

The God of Abraham, and of Isaac, and of Jacob, the God of our fathers, hath glorified His Son Jesus.[16]

Therefore it is of faith, that it might be by grace; to the end the promise might be sure to all the seed; not to that only which is of the law, but to that also which is of the faith of Abraham; who is the father of us all, (As it is written, I have made thee a father of many nations,) before him whom he believed, even God, who quickeneth the dead, and calleth those things which be not as though they were.[17]

Many times in Scripture we find references to the fathers of Israel. These verses are usually written citing the "fathers" as a source of authority or as a right to blessing through relationship. When the roots of the Israelite people are traced back through Jacob, we always find Abraham at the source. It is he who entered into a higher relationship with God through faith.

It is Abraham who finds connection through Melchizedek all the way back to Adam. It is Abraham to whom Levi paid tithes establishing a doorway to unlock spiritual promises for us. Abraham and his son and their sons speak to us of establishing father/son order into the generations. He is the father of us all, thereby signifying that we can have a place in his generations.

Abraham was persuaded of the promises God had made and embraced them but never received them, except by faith, knowing they were yet a long way off. Isaac was a kind of down payment or first fruit of an innumerable number of heirs that would come from his loins. As much of a blessing and joy as Isaac must have been to aging Sarah and Abraham, he had to become a father if the promises made to Abraham were to come to pass.

Isaac must pass on to his sons those things that were given to him. He would not only have to pass them on but do it in such a way as to be convinced that he would have at least one son who would pass it on to his sons as well. The promise of the seed of Abraham becoming a nation could only happen after the promises had been passed down through the fourth generation.

The Significance of the Fourth Generation

This was the word of the Lord which He spake unto Jehu, saying, Thy sons shall sit on the throne of Israel unto the fourth generation. And so it came to pass.[18]

But in the fourth generation they shall come hither again: for the iniquity of the Amorites is not yet full.[19]

The Lord is longsuffering, and of great mercy, forgiving iniquity and transgression, and by no means clearing the guilty, visiting the iniquity of the fathers upon the children unto the third and fourth generation.[20]

A vision that is not passed down to the fourth generation will never become perpetual. It is through the fourth generation that God establishes the nation. God blessed Jehu for executing justice on the house of Ahab. Because of this, God promised Jehu that his sons would sit on the throne of Israel unto the fourth generation. It was a way of showing that God was willing to establish his generations.

Jehu's unwillingness to walk in the way of the Lord ensured that the promise would die with the fourth generation. God had promised him a legacy, but he had nothing but corruption to pass down to his offspring. God visited Jehu's iniquity unto the fourth generation. After this, none of his descendants sat on the throne. They lost their right to rulership because their generations were perverted.

God made promises to other people in the Bible, not just to the Hebrews. He had a plan with the Amorites as well. The iniquity of the Amorites was not yet full; that is, it had not yet completely permeated all their generations. Even though God knew what was going to happen, He waited until iniquity was completed in the Amorite people.

God promises Abraham that in the fourth generation after their leaving the land his descendants would return. On returning to the promised land, God uses the Israelites to destroy King Sihon and the Amorites. One people had completely passed out of the will of God while another was entering its promise after four generations of absence.

Three times we are told that God would visit *"the iniquity of the fathers upon the children unto the third and fourth generation."* He will show mercy to thousands who love Him and keep His commandments. This is telling us that traits of fathers whether good or bad are passed on through the generations. This is often referred to as generational curses or blessings. This is not God punishing the children for the sins of the parents. Rather the word *visit* implies that God would look upon, or witness, the passing of iniquity in the generations and wait to pronounce punishment.

The fourth generation brought judgment in Jehu's family but blessing in Israel's, thus instructing us on the importance of making our ministries generational. The qualification of our continuing ministries and visions only happens in the fourth generation. This is at a time when we are either no longer alive or no longer able to personally influence what our sons will have made out of the inheritance we have given them. No matter how gifted or powerful our ministries may be, they will wane and vanish unless we are wise enough to govern their progression through the generations.

> *And the things that thou hast heard of me among many witnesses, the same commit thou to faithful men, who shall be able to teach others also.*[21]

In the New Testament as well, Paul speaks to this son encouraging him to pass his doctrine to following generations. The things of Paul (first generation) that were given to Timothy (second generation) were to be committed to faithful men (third generation) who would be able to teach others (fourth generation). The word "commit" (*paratithemi*) means to deposit as a trust or deposit for protection. The second generation cannot just explain his father's vision; he must put it into the third generation in such a way that he can trust them with its safekeeping. Paul understood the necessity of passing on vision and purpose through the fourth generation.

Ordering the Church in Its Generations

Abraham was the first generation of promise. The promises were made to him. Isaac was the second generation. The promises were passed on through him. Jacob was the third generation; the promises began to be established in him. In the fourth generation there was a manifestation into the 12 tribes of Israel. Each generation is different and growing. Each possesses the promises and vision of the previous generation. Abraham, Isaac, and Jacob are not only fathers to their direct sons but also fathers of an entire nation that grew up in the successful transference of the inheritance from their generations to the nation.

In every church there are generations. A ministry needs to become generational if it is to be completed. The Lord desires to help us order the generations within our churches. Each generation is different and fulfills a particular part of the vision given through the set ministry. Abraham had a son, grandsons, and many great-grandsons. His family was ordered and growing, with each generation being unique.

In a local church, the set minister can be looked on as the first generation. He receives the vision from the Lord that is to be established in the house. He is the one who comes to a new land and forges the work in the adversity of untried opportunities and unknown destinations. He is a father of all who follow that vision, just as Abraham was a father to all Israel.

Just as Abraham was not the literal or direct father of all Israel but only of his literal offspring Isaac, so the set minister is not the direct ministry father of all in church but only of those sons God has put directly under him in relationship. These sons are confirmed by the Spirit and tested through the process of time and trial. They become the second generation of the work.

It is the desire of every well-adjusted father to see his sons bring forth another generation. Grandparents long for grandchildren. Set ministries should long to see the day when sons grow to the maturity to bring forth a third generation of the work. It is only an insecure and degenerate father who would castrate a son. These are deficient fathers who fear competition and desire a following rather than a family.

One reason ministry fathers long to see the third generation is that the third generation is evidence of their success in passing down ministry through a son. They become the sign to the ministry grandfather that his seed will continue in the earth and his purpose will be completed.

> *A good man leaveth an inheritance to his children's children: and the wealth of the sinner is laid up for the just.*[22]

> *Children's children are the crown of old men; and the glory of children are their fathers.*[23]

The inheritance of fathers is not just for children but also for grandchildren. If ministry grandchildren are in right order then the effectiveness of the grandfather's ability to establish perpetual father/son order is confirmed.

When we are in the thick of raising our own children and instituting our own careers and futures, we think little of grandchildren. When we are established and matured, the future of our adult children and the desire to see them have children are of primary concern. Mature ministry seeks mature sons who will become fathers.

It is second generation sons who have the responsibility of not only bringing forth the third generation but instructing them and equipping them to establish a fourth generation in right order. We have already discussed the importance of ministry being carried to the fourth generation. Just as the nation of Israel consisted of many tribes, likewise does the Church. God may break down the holy nation, so to speak, into tribes. A patriarchal ministry that is successful in establishing vision and purpose to the fourth generation can be thought of as a tribe or an extended family of that vision. In the fourth generation our visions are multiplied and take on permanence.

Abraham had only one son, but it was all he needed. We in ministry may have multiple sons, but even if we are able to pass our vision on to just one loyal and trained son, our vision will continue and become completed. It is the first generation that has the greatest natural struggle. Abraham has to move out of paganism into a new place. He witnesses the death of his father before he is able to move into the land. He will journey to many places and struggle with many people.

The land of inheritance would pass to others before it would be restored to his generations. Like first generation ministry, he is on the move charting new territory, learning to take dominion over the inheritance. He will be tested in his willingness to offer his blessing, his promise, and his future to God. In the offering of his son, he will be found unwavering, blameless, and completely faithful. In the training of his son for inheritance, he will be found totally without defect.

Isaac is the second generation. He must be found willing not only to receive the inheritance, but also to pass it on to a faithful son. It takes Isaac 20 years to have a child. He is 60 years old when he becomes a father. It is only when Rebecca said, "I want a child, Isaac. Talk to the Lord!" that she conceived. It would seem he was not overly motivated to produce an offspring, yet it was the only way to secure the promises for his father and himself. It is perhaps one characteristic of the second generation: They are not usually motivated to take on the responsibility of calling out a third generation.

Isaac lives in the inheritance of his father. He will learn to recover some things lost to Abraham and add to the inheritance as well. He unstops some wells dug by his father and digs some new ones himself. He has learned to follow his father. He is willing to trust Abraham completely. He was not a young boy when Abraham went to the sacrifice. Abraham may have been willing to offer his son; but Isaac, whose life was in question, was willing to follow and be obedient to his father even in the face of death! This is dedication. This is the trust that second generation sons must have in their fathers.

He has learned so well from his father that when faced with similar circumstances he reacts in similar ways as the story of King Abimelech illustrates. He chooses his wife at the direction of his father. As an adult he lives in his father's house and learns his father's business. This is the submission of a true son who lives totally in the vision and purpose of his father.

Isaac has two sons. Esau (whose name means "red like clay") is a man of the earth. He is a great hunter. He knows the ways of the world and has learned to walk in those ways. His heart is toward the world. Jacob is mama's boy. He grabs the heel of his brother at birth. He wants inheritance and he wants blessing and he'll position himself to receive both. Esau being of the earth is fleshly. He'll sell his birthright for whatever feeds the flesh.

Sometimes a good father has trouble distinguishing between his sons. Sometimes it takes outside intervention for the father to pass on inheritance to the rightful son. Abraham has one son but Isaac has two sons. There must be a division between that which is of the earth and that which is of Heaven in the third generation.

In ministry the second generation is going to have to make a division between that which is natural and that which is spiritual. Like Isaac they are going to have to forsake what may be their first choice motivated out of comfort and personal preference for the bestowing of blessing on that which is chosen by God. Esau and Jacob also speak of the division or separation of thought that must occur within ministry so that the things from Heaven may dominate over the things that are of the earth.

Jacob is the third generation. He is abundantly blessed just by dwelling in the land his father and grandfather forged in their efforts to establish a family. The family plan is well laid. His wife will come from the same line as the wives of his forefathers. His business will be a family business. He is the third generation, so he will excel abundantly. He is blessed. He is a type of a higher dimension. He sees the face of God at Peniel. He visits the house of God at Bethel. He grows to know the God of the house at Bethel. He views the gate of Heaven and understands the operation of bringing heavenly things to earth. God hears and answers Jacob.

Jacob learns from his fathers. Like his grandfather, he builds an altar at the house of God. Like his father, he takes his wives from relation. Like his fathers, he is on a journey. He does not stay in one place. His blessings are multiplied. And like his fathers, he learns the art of deception.

As with Jacob's family, we in ministry can pass on to our sons not only our strengths but also our weaknesses, if left unresolved. Abraham deceives Abimelech; Isaac deceives Abimelech; Jacob deceives Isaac and Laban; and his sons perform the ultimate deception to Jacob when they tell him his son Joseph is dead. It is also the deception of his Uncle Laban that will lead to Jacob's having sons from four different women.

Jacob has his own struggles, but they are different from those of his fathers. He is established through the inheritance of Abraham and Isaac. But he is prepared for change by spiritual contests that will leave him enlarged, strengthened, and ready for God. His flesh may limp but his spirit has soared to new heights. His name will be changed. He is no longer "Jacob," a supplanter, but "Israel," which means one having power with God. His name would become the name of a nation. It is from this third generation that the children are greatly increased in number. These children will become the fourth generation.

Jacob's male children numbered 12. Twelve is a number of government and foundation. It is in this fourth generation of promise that foundations will be established. These sons will become the 12 tribes of Israel. They will all flourish in numbers of descendants. They will go down into Egypt as a family but will come out as a great nation.

> *Seeing that Abraham shall surely become a great and mighty nation, and all the nations of the earth shall be blessed in him.*[24]

Their children will learn to dwell together and work together and be in bondage together and eventually learn to fight for one another so that each could obtain a portion of the land of their forefathers. This generation will give its father many joys and much heartache. This is a generation of sons all having the same father but different mothers. This may speak of ministry sons who come out of various systems but are united by relationship with a common father. Their children will be known as the nation of Israel. In them and those of us who carry on as this nation, the promise of the Lord to Abraham will be realized. All the nations of the earth will be blessed through the holy nation made up of the people of God.

> *And thou shalt say unto Pharaoh, Thus saith the Lord, Israel is My **son**, even My firstborn.*[25]

God will call the nation Israel by the singular title: "son." The entire nation is a son of God. The many membered Body of Christ and the holy nation of God are likewise called by a singular title: "man-child" in Revelation 12:5 and a "son" in Revelation 21:7. This is what the perfection of our righteous generations is destined to produce.

In many ways the events in the lives of Abraham and his generations are allegories for the ordering of the generations of the church. The set ministry is the first generation of a church. He may be the second or third generation of someone else's ministry, but within that local setting he becomes the first generation. In one sense, we are all many generations. We are the first generation of our fathers; we are the second generation of our grandfathers; but in the local church, if we are the set minister, we become the first generation of that work.

Like Abraham we are sojourners in a strange land, inheritors of promises and a work of God. We don't always have a clear view on the future. We don't understand all aspects of our ministries. The Lord wants to birth a son through us but we're not exactly sure how this will happen.

Sometimes in our failure to fully comprehend the path the Lord would take to complete the promise, we try to help Him out. Some things just seem to make such good natural sense that we're sure this is the way the Lord would want to accomplish His plan. When we miss the mark, we have to learn to let go of our weakness but not His promise. In time we learn to find joy in the process of trusting God and living for His purpose and not our desires.

Our ministry hope is that the work He has given us may be completed. We see the necessity of raising a son. If we can raise just one son in complete submission to the vision, who will give life to other generations, then we know that there will be a fulfillment of the things we've believed.

To raise this son, we will ourselves have to be in order. We will have to see sons as a blessing from the Lord and not as people who draw from our energies and infringe on our limited time.

In rearing sons, we will have to become adept at dealing with all levels of maturity and handling all varieties of problems. In this we will find it is more blessed to give than to receive. Sons teach us how to sacrifice, discipline, and love more perfectly. Sons, in some ways, become the greatest instruments the Lord can use to teach us about ourselves.

Like Isaac, the second generation of church ministry must be in complete submission. They must be totally willing to subordinate their agenda to the vision of their father. Nothing short of death should separate them from a righteous father's business. Sons in order are the evidence of successful ministry. This generation will have to sort between those desiring true relationship and those who only seek association. When we see that our purpose can be completed in no other way, we will do all that is necessary to bring this generation to maturity.

Like Jacob, the third generation of the church will be the offspring of the second generation, not the first. A set ministry must be willing to allow *mature* sons to bring forth sons of their own. We are not in competition with our sons but in a cooperative effort to establish generations and fulfill purpose. Set ministry should help its sons mature into fatherhood, learn the order of rearing sons, and provide necessary counsel and insight as needed. The set ministry is ever cognizant of passing on purpose, identity, and vision so that the fourth generation—the generation which will secure the foundations of the fathers—may be one in vision and order with the first generation.

The Set Ministry's Role in Establishing the Generations

It is the set ministry's responsibility for raising the foundations of many generations within his house. He must assess the maturity of his own sons and those who would be sons of those sons. He must see to it that he does not have a situation where immature children are trying to be fathers to other children. This is a curse of our society in the natural and religious systems. Infant sons, due to a lack of physical ability, cannot give seed. Adolescent sons, due to a lack of maturity, should not give seed.

But mature sons should not fail to give seed or the generations cannot be perpetuated.

One error that some make in trying to establish father/son order is that they teach this order in such a way that all in church feel they need to be fathers, now! Most are probably not ready. Some may never be fathers. Since most churches have not ordered their generations, the set ministry should thoroughly educate the local church concerning this teaching while providing private instruction to sons on the more in-depth matters related to father/son order.

The people should be encouraged to pray for this order to be established in the Church. They should be taught to be at peace in allowing it to happen, giving the whole Church time to grow. After all, it is God that puts fathers and sons together—not man. If they understand and accept this, they will have a common goal to work toward and an understanding of how their ministry fits in the purpose of the Church. If we are not careful, we can have the saints scurrying about looking for fathers and seeking after sons. Father/son order requires maturity. Maturity requires time. Those who have not matured as sons should not be fathers.

The third generation must come from the second. This means the set minister's sons need to be called out first. They must be trained in father/son issues. They must be found faithful as sons. They must hear the voice of God confirming their calling forth into sons. They must grow into full maturity. They must be committed to the process. They must feel the Spirit turning their heart toward sons.

This all takes time. In fact, since the second generation is often sluggish in regards to this, it may be that there are numbers of people in church who understand and are of a maturity to come into order before their fathers are prepared to call them forth. Or it may be that this teaching may confirm to many in a spiritual church what the Lord has been witnessing to them for some time.

The set minister may of necessity have to nurture these, much as a grandfather giving care to a grandson. In the Spirit it is evident whom God has aligned with whom. We as set ministry cannot choose who should be the sons to which fathers; that is the Spirit's job.

We can and should, however, confirm to our sons their choices before the next generation is called forth. Remember, it is better not to call forth sons than to call them forth and let them languish in adolescence because their fathers are not mature enough to provide proper care. It is a father who calls sons—he should do it in the wisdom of the Spirit—and a son does not choose or call a father in ministry any more than in the natural world.

Fathers and sons are not set in order according to physical age. A younger father may very well have an older son. It also does not depend upon how long someone has been in the church. A person who has been in church ten years could be the son of someone who has only been in the house for four years. If we heed the Spirit, He will order our generations, and if not, all attempts will only be the work of man. We can take any spiritual principle and subject it to religious laws, traditions, and lack of maturity.

Recognizing Sons

Recognizing who is a father to a particular son is really a work of the Spirit. It cannot be a product of our natural understanding. Sons are not necessarily those we've brought to the Lord or those to whom we are drawn in fellowship. They may or may not be those with whom we have a lot in common or with whom we have like callings and gifting. There are several tests we can use to help us judge these relationships.

First: **Maturity**. Sons won't always be mature, but fathers must be. If a saint is not mature (meaning trained, in right order, and submitted to his father), there is no purpose in trying to discern who may be his sons. We don't look for young children or teenagers to produce sons in the natural world, so why would we look for this within the church?

Second: **The test of time.** Time is a great aid in ordering all types of relationships. Relationships of true fathers to true sons need time to develop and endure. Right relationships will stand the test of time. When calling forth sons, don't make rash judgments or accept sons because of their need for a father. Take time to observe and seek after the Spirit's witness. Time will tell.

Third: **Sons are drawn out of the same vision.** If someone who desires to be your son cannot relate fully to your vision, then he is not your son, or at least not a legitimate son. To become a father, he will have to first have a vision that comes forth from your vision. If there is no agreement as to vision, there can be no development of father/son relationship.

Fourth: **Family and not just associates.** We may have meaningful and loving relationships with many people but there is a distinctive bond, in the natural as well as the spiritual, between a father and his son. Make sure that tie exists. Father/son relationships are family relationships. To be a son, one must be drawn to the father and his ministry family.

Fifth: **Identity.** Natural fathers have common features with sons. Their sons often look like, sound like, and act like their father. They are not carbon copies, but anyone can notice the similarities. So it should be with ministry sons. In sons the call, purpose, and operation of God may be distinct, but the heart, as pertaining to vision and desire, should be the same as the father's heart.

Sixth: **Proceeding word.** Does the father have a proceeding word from God that gives shape to the son's ministry and purpose? Does a son receive it as such and does it produce its intended result?

Seventh: **The confirmation of our father.** Does our father or the set ministry, confirm the sons we would call forth? Does our father recognize the people we would have be sons to us as actual sons?

Eighth: **The acknowledgment of the Spirit.** Has the Spirit confirmed this relationship? He, after all, is the one who calls the generations according to His purpose. If we do not have the confirmation of the Spirit, we should not enter into relationships as either a father or a son in ministry.

Other Biblical Patterns

Whereby are given unto us exceeding great and precious promises: that by these ye might be partakers of the divine nature, having escaped the corruption that is in the world through lust.[26]

Divine order through restored generations connects us to the promises God gave Abraham. As Christians we are not just here to "go to Heaven" and to see that others do likewise, but we have a great purpose far beyond what many have even realized or sought to find. In addition to purpose, we have an even greater divine destiny. Bible promises allow us to be partakers of the divine nature!

Purpose is vitally important, but it is not as great as destiny. Our purpose should be leading us toward our destiny. Purpose can be sterile without destiny. We can have purpose without destiny. A door has important purpose, to provide protection and privacy, but it has no destiny beyond its purpose. Our destiny is related to our heavenly Father; but ministry fathers help to give us focus and understanding leading to our destiny.

Abraham and his generations are perhaps the most typical example of generational order, yet many other biblical patterns could be cited. Moses, Joshua, and the tribes of Israel; Jesus, Paul, and Titus; Samuel, Saul, and Jonathan; David, Solomon, and Rehoboam; Elijah, Elisha, and Gehazi and others give us insight into father/son relationships.

Much could be said about the above generations. A more in-depth study of these gives a clearer understanding of how to establish generations and pass on inheritance. One thing we would discover if we studied their generational order is that none of the above was established into the fourth generation.

In Samuel and Saul we would see what happens to a father who has an illegitimate son. In Jonathan and Saul we see how a righteous son should follow an unrighteous father. In David we see what happens when we become a son-*in-law* to a father-*in-law*. We learn of a father-*in-law's* heart and the rights and proper responses of a son-*in-law* to an oppressive situation. We see how sons in such a circumstance seek to establish new spiritual order.

David, Solomon, and Rehoboam instruct us on the necessity of rearing sons naturally and spiritually. If we don't establish and pass on father/son order properly, our work will become divided and inheritance will be wasted, just as the Kingdom of Israel was divided in Rehoboam's reign. Elijah and Elisha of course are a perfect example of establishing right order. Every issue related to father/son order has a perfect example in Scripture.

The Blessing of Double Portions and Continuing Inheritance

The Lord wants us to come up out of our single-portion blessings to live in double portions. This will be the result of generations set in order. God gives to us and has given to great men and woman, past and present, powerful single portions of ministry and power. In these single portions great Christians have established churches, taken authority in the spirit world, and done many wonderful works. Their testimonies leave many hungering for similar power and effect within their personal ministries. It is the Lord's desire to give us, not similar, but greater expressions of the Spirit. For this to happen we must be like Elisha who ordered his life to receive the double portion.

> *And the sons of the prophets that were at Bethel came forth to Elisha, and said unto him, Knowest thou that the Lord will take away thy master from thy head to day? And he said, Yea, I know it; hold ye your peace.*[27]

> *For the Father loveth the Son, and showeth Him all things that Himself doeth: and He will show Him greater works than these, that ye may marvel.*[28]

> *Verily, verily, I say unto you, He that believeth on Me, the works that I do shall he do also; and greater works than these shall he do; because I go unto My Father.*[29]

> *And it came to pass, when they were gone over, that Elijah said unto Elisha, Ask what I shall do for thee, before I be taken away from thee. And Elisha said, I pray thee, let a double portion of thy spirit be upon me.*[30]

There were many prophets in the days of Elijah but only one who followed him as a son. These prophets understood spiritual things. They could see what was about to happen. They knew the time of Elijah's departure, but only one, Elisha, was willing against all obstacles to put himself "eye to eye" in his father's ministry. The prophets had association with Elijah but Elisha has relationship. He will do twice the recorded miracles as his father. The double portion will give him the inheritance of his father added to his own ministry, making him twice as powerful and twice as effective. Sons should be greater than the father.

Because we live in single portions, in Christianity we are forever trying to reinvent the wheel, so to speak—always trying to get back to the ministry of the early Church in power, influence, and effect. Yet in truth, we should be far beyond this. One generation receives from the Lord and walks in the grace given it. It does a work only to have its inheritance lost or put into religious systems that squander it and conform it after men rather than God. Each generation for the most part has to start over.

For almost 2,000 years the Church has been living without double portions—inheriting the traditions and disorder of men rather than the ministry of fathers. Jesus tells us that greater works came to Him from the Father. He also said His people would do greater works because He was going to the Father—not greater because there are more people doing the works but greater works in power and effect. He was speaking of double portions, which the Church for the most part has not yet walked in because it has not ordered itself in the generations.

Jesus said we would do greater works. This is because those after Him would inherit His ministry and power and be able to add it to the ministry and power that God gave them. It would have a doubling effect. This is progression of power and ministry in us. Just think if those things given the early Church had been continually handed down through the generations, increasing in power and effectiveness with each subsequent generation. How great would the Church today be?

Paul would have passed on his inheritance to Timothy. Timothy would walk not only in what God gave him but what was added to him through Paul. Timothy's ministry sons would have not only what God gave the son but also what Timothy passed on in inheritance, which would have included what Timothy received from

Paul. If this would have carried down to us through the generations, how powerful would the Church be today after 50 such generations?

If the set ministry passes on inheritance to sons, they receive not only their own ministry in God but that of their father as well. The second generation becomes mightier than the first, the third mightier than the second, and the fourth generation will have the accumulated inheritance of all the previous generations. This requires us to receive and pass on inheritance in proper order. What is manifested in the third generation becomes established in the fourth. If we reestablish this order to the third even the fourth generation, then and only then can it become perpetual.

In the natural world, if the generation that receives inheritance does not spend it but uses it for the benefit of the following generation, then that third generation inherits not only the possessions the parents were able to accumulate but also those given through the grandparents. This is how the fortunes of families like the Fords have been passed on through the generations. A member of the Ford family has sat on the board of directors of Ford Motor Company for the last four generations. They didn't squander the inheritance but passed it on.

Now in the natural world, if a person receives an inheritance and foolishly wastes it at the gambling casino or on short-lived material possessions, then he will have nothing of that inheritance to give to his children. If, however, he puts that inheritance to proper use, investing it and building upon it, he will be able to give the next generation not only the estate he has acquired but also that which was given him from his father. If each ministry generation followed this order there would be no limit to the increase of its power and domain.

To make this happen in the church requires great diligence and understanding in ordering the Church in its generations. One thing that can be noticed from studying examples of passing large inheritances is how each generation deals with inheritance in a different way. The first generation had to go through much struggle and adversity in acquiring the inheritance. The second generation knew what it cost their father and would usually have respect unto the inheritance, using it sparingly. The third generation received the inheritance. It cost them nothing, and more often than not they were willing to live off the inheritance. By the time it was passed on through the fourth generation, in many cases, it was so diluted that it disappeared.

Where are the fortunes established by Diamond Jim Brady, Andrew Carnegie, Thomas Edison, and Alexander Graham Bell? However they were eventually distributed, these inheritances did not increase through the generations. In like manner, the spiritual inheritance passed down in the Church for the last two millennia has dissipated rather than having been increased.

The authors of the New Testament have indeed handed down to all in Christianity a great inheritance of scriptural truth but not necessarily their ministry. Where are the ministry inheritances of Paul and Apollos and thousands of other great saints down through the ages? The spirit of these ministries may be revived in the reestablishment of father/son order.

Historically, however, they have been consumed by religion rather than increased through sons. This is why the message of father/son order is so powerful. It is not about a man or a mission or a single ministry but about an order that will bring forth the generation of Christ, empowered with every spiritual gift and blessing of its Father, Jesus Christ.

ENDNOTES

1. Psalm 102:16.
2. Psalm 102:18.
3. Ezra 2:62.
4. Isaiah 53:8.

THE ORDER OF A *Son*

5. Psalm 22:30.
6. Matthew 1:17.
7. 1 Corinthians 15:23.
8. Galatians 5:24.
9. Romans 8:19.
10. Acts 3:25.
11. Luke 1:55.
12. Galatians 3:29.
13. Genesis 18:19.
14. Exodus 3:6.
15. 2 Kings 13:23.
16. Acts 3:13.
17. Romans 4:16-17.
18. 2 Kings 15:12.
19. Genesis 15:16.
20. Numbers 14:18.
21. 2 Timothy 2:2.
22. Proverbs 13:22.
23. Proverbs 17:6.
24. Genesis 18:18.
25. Exodus 4:22.
26. 2 Peter 1:4.
27. 2 Kings 2:3.
28. John 5:20.
29. John 14:12.
30. 2 Kings 2:9.

CHAPTER SIX

GAINING DIRECTION
THROUGH SETTING GOALS

A desire to receive and walk in God's direction is a constant that is ever present in the Christian life. Regardless of our position in Christ or the length of our service, without an ability to understand and follow the direction of the Lord, we will be hindered in completing the full will of God for our ministries. Uncountable sermons have been preached and a profusion of materials have been published as to various avenues available to the Christian in gaining the direction of God.

The abundance of such gives witness to the desire of every minister of God to know the Lord's direction for his or her ministry. Without question such direction is tied up with our personal relationship with Jesus. Prayer, knowledge of the Word, and the ability to hear the voice of the Spirit as well as the voice of godly counsel, all have a significant part in each saint's quest for godly direction. There is a practical side as well to acquiring such direction.

Godly direction can be thought of as not only understanding the will of God but also knowing how we are to accomplish that will. Ministerial direction is the supernatural guidance of our actions and conduct so as to bring forth His will in our ministries. As the apostle Paul writes; *"Be ye not unwise, but understanding what the will of the Lord is.*"¹ We need to be wise in knowing His will and understanding how to accomplish it. This is the essence of godly direction. Unfortunately, many of God's people lack a practical method for bringing His full and continued direction to pass.

Too many think that godly direction involves nothing more than praying and doing what the Lord speaks. It does begin with godly communication, but this alone will not cause a believer to fully receive or walk in that direction. There are many reasons for this.

We may not be completely open to hear. We may have hindrances from the flesh and from tradition. We may not be fully committed to acting on His leading. We may not be in complete spiritual order. We may not know how to do what He is asking, or we may not be connected in ministry or vision to a father. Receiving and walking in godly direction requires practical steps.

A friend of mine relayed to me that in his early Christian life he would often attend church services and hear many wonderful sermons from many wonderful men of God. They would speak on knowing God, on God's plan for mankind, on receiving the promises of God, on the power of the Holy Spirit, on the need to live a righteous life, and on many other marvelous topics. They would speak on what he likes to call the "what" of Christian preaching, but very little on the "why" and almost nothing about the "how to."

Many times the longing for understanding that was in him made him want to stand up and shout, "What you are saying is awesome and inspiring but HOW CAN I BRING IT TO PASS IN MY LIFE? DON'T JUST TELL ME ABOUT JESUS AND BIBLE PROMISES AND THE GREAT THINGS THAT ARE SOON TO HAPPEN, BUT TELL ME *HOW*!"

"How shall these things be" was Mary's response to the angelic news. The closest most could come, in answering how, was to admonish their congregations to "Pray! Stop listening to the

enemy! Believe God! Be obedient! Trust and have faith!" and of course an almost universal answer in every situation, "Tithe!"

Such answers have become almost clichés, as the doctor who tells his patient, "Take two aspirins and call me in the morning." These sorts of answers can give a real "spiritual headache" to someone seeking to know the "how" of godly direction. Knowing the "how" is one of six fundamental, universal, spiritual questions all in every culture ask. It became apparent that most were well meaning but had never answered the "how" as it pertained to godly direction.

Too often Christians fail to see the practical application of life in the Spirit. If God promises them a new car, some think it shows a lack of faith to work overtime in order to have the money to purchase it. To some, the spiritual realm is little more than binding and loosing, commanding and demanding, and letting the devil know who's in charge. Some have never considered that going to work or washing the dishes may be a very spiritual activity. It has never occurred to some that taking authority over the enemy and walking in God's will may involve personal changes and a willingness to allow God's process to establish in us a natural as well as spiritual order.

The remainder of this chapter is not intended to list all there is to know about godly direction or even a large portion. What are listed are a few practical approaches to growing in godly direction. As is often the case in gaining spiritual understanding, we don't have to know a great deal about any given subject, but if we apply ourselves to the little we do understand, great and awesome vistas of His truth are opened unto us. With the right application not only do we gain knowledge but, more importantly, we gain understanding that brings us into order and the clear direction of God.

Spiritual Goal Setting

In the world of business and in the business of self-improvement much is made of goal setting, and for an important reason: It works!

Statements such as "Plan your work and work your plan," and "We don't plan to fail; we fail to plan," have become common axioms in our culture for the simple truths they contain. Christian ministry is not conditioned upon being successful in business, but it is conditioned upon successfully *ordering* our ministries according to biblical principles and patterns.

These principles and patterns were established by many other notable biblical characters and even Jesus Himself. It's a surprise to some that many of the noteworthy Bible leaders demonstrated a plan and a method for accomplishing that plan (goals) in their ministries. They didn't just wake up in the morning and say, "Okay, God, what's next?"

Harvard University did a study in 1953. The study showed that only three percent of the graduating students wrote down their specific career goals. Now most, if not all, graduates tend to have goals such as a good job, a nice home, time and money for travel, and the like, but if goals (like vision) are not written down they tend to become wishful thinking rather than attainable objectives. Twenty years later researchers interviewed that class of 1953 and found that the three percent who wrote down their goals were worth more than the other 97 percent combined. Not that material wealth should be the mark of our ministries, but completed vision and ministerial order must be and they require a biblical plan and method to bring them to pass.

The ministries of Moses, Nehemiah, Jesus, and others show the need for establishing a plan and a method to accomplish that plan in our ministries. They are a pattern for those of us to follow in completing our ministries. There was a method to the way these men understood the will of God and accomplished the work given them. Because they were in order they can become a pattern for us as Paul writes, *"Howbeit for this cause I obtained mercy, that in me first Jesus Christ might show forth all longsuffering, for a pattern to them which should hereafter believe on Him to life everlasting.*"[2] Not only was he a pattern but his sons were to provide one as well, as Paul exhorts Titus, "*In all things showing thyself a pattern.*"[3]

Fathers establish patterns for sons. A ministry father's vision becomes the wellspring from which sons must draw their individual visions. It is impossible to speak about spiritual goals without first understanding something about vision. Most ministries equate vision with the promises of God. This is why the way some ministries speak of visions sounds similar to the following: "We are going to win this city for Christ and show the power of the Holy Spirit to all in need," or "The Lord is going to spread our ministry through home fellowships and programs for the needy and as we seek to help the lost they will see the love of God."

These may be godly promises if they come from Him, but they are not really visions. Unless a church has a well-defined vision from God the saints will have difficulty in setting and accomplishing spiritual goals for their individual ministries. (See Chapter Four for more on ministry vision.)

Accomplishing the vision given to each of us from the Lord involves setting written spiritual goals. As any godly vision must be written and clear in order for it to become completed and generational, so spiritual goals must be put down on paper if they are to be effective. A goal that is not in written form is not a goal at all but a wish. Since the foundation of all spiritual goals finds its source in godly vision, the first step to setting such goals is breaking down the vision into its basic parts. What are the parts of the vision and what goals will lead to completing its various parts?

*I press toward the **mark** for the **prize** of the high calling of God in Christ Jesus.*[4]

*The **plan** pleased me well; so I took twelve of your men, one man from each tribe.*[5]

*And He came to Nazareth, where He had been brought up: and, as His **custom** was, He went into the synagogue on the sabbath day, and stood up for to read.*[6]

*Know ye not that they which **run** in a race **run all**, but one receiveth the **prize**? **So run, that ye may obtain.**[7]*

The above Scriptures speak of the need to do things in order, according to a plan, with a prescribed goal or result in mind. The apostle Paul had set a mark (goal) before him. It was the thing that gave direction to his ministry. All he did in God was in one way or another linked to achieving the goal of the high calling of God in Christ Jesus.

When Moses sent the 12 spies into the promised land it was according to a plan. He was given a vision by God of leading His people into a land of promise. To do this Moses had to in some manner establish goals, such as the suggestion to survey of the land. This goal led to a plan to send forth spies, one from each tribe, to check out the land and bring a report of what they found. In the episode there is a lesson to be learned about not having people committed to the vision of God-given leadership. Because of fear, the people were turned against the vision.

A plan lists the details of how we are to accomplish stated goals. Bible leaders always had a plan from which they worked. Setting goals forces us to communicate with God on establishing plans that will bring those goals to pass. It clarifies God's direction and helps us understand His timing and the steps we are to take.

Ministries without goals are ministries without an effective plan for bringing God's will to pass through their work. Even in the ministry of Jesus we see He didn't minister randomly but had a method or plan as indicated by the phrase "as His custom was." The Gospels teach us that He had a plan or a method to His ministry. All Christians are involved in a race but only those who run the race effectively will achieve the object of the race: the prize. Establishing spiritual goals helps us to achieve the prize.

God has given all His people great and precious promises, but not all His people obtain all the promises of God meant for them. This is not because they don't have a right to these promises but because they don't walk in a God-given plan that would bring those promises to pass in their lives. Bible personalities are continually directing us in the formation of goals and an ordered plan for life and ministry. Jesus in the Sermon on the Mount, Paul in his exhortations to his son in First Timothy chapter 2, Peter in his direction to the church in Second Peter chapter 1, all speak of establishing patterns in the Christian life. Many sections of Scripture similar to these are given to us as a means to give the believer direction, order, and the achievement of spiritual goals.

The Book of Nehemiah recounts the history of a man who had a vision from God to rebuild the walls of Jerusalem and to reestablish a consecrated people in the land. The work of ministry must always start with a clear vision—a vision not of man but of God. As you read the history of this particular event, you'll notice that Nehemiah had to have established some goals and a plan to bring them to pass. He had many goals. One of his goals was to go to Jerusalem and oversee the work, another was to gain the aid of King Artaxerxes.

These goals led him to establishing plans to bring them to pass. He had a plan in how he was going to come before the king. When he was granted permission to return to Jerusalem, he had a plan. He didn't just say thank you and wonder about what he should do next; but he knew exactly what he wanted from the king.

His plan included asking for protection and letter of passage from the king; it also included the king's granting him materials necessary to complete the task. He had thought it through. He had a plan because he had spiritual goals based upon godly vision. Without the establishment of goals and plans to bring them to pass, the walls of Jerusalem and the reconsecration of the people would never have come to pass.

Some Benefits to Establishing Spiritual Goals

Spiritual goals help us address our fears. Fear is the opposite of faith. When we lack certainty about who we are in Christ or what it is we should be doing, when we lack direction and understanding, we open ourselves up to various kinds of fear. When we see progress toward accomplishing our spiritual goals, it builds faith. We have a clarity about our ministries and a confidence about those things the Lord is speaking to us.

Spiritual goals help us avoid procrastination. Procrastination delays the process of God in our lives and causes frustration in our ministries. Written goals give us a clear list of what needs to come to pass through our ministries. They establish a timetable for action and we never have to wonder what it is that we should be doing. They keep us focused and help keep us out of a daydream existence.

Spiritual goals help us break down our visions into workable segments. Visions by their nature encompass a large work and require time to be brought to completion. If we are not able to break down our visions into manageable portions, we may become discouraged and lose heart. As we are able to accomplish our goals we will see little by little the achievement of our vision.

Spiritual goals help us keep from being distracted. Paul tells us that there are, *"Many kinds of voices in the world, and none of them is without signification."*[7] Many things are continually speaking to us. They are often important things. The daily activities of life are constantly drawing on each of us. There are many good things we could be doing. In fact we can get so busy in doing good things that we fail to do the better things and even fail to do those things which are most important for our ministries. Goals keep us focused. Goals help us have confidence that our ministries will become completed and ongoing.

Spiritual goals help give those associated with our ministry the ability to see their part in the work. Leaders need to give people direction. It is impossible to give adequate direction without goals. People need well-defined goals so they can clearly see the objective and understand how the vision of the church will be accomplished. This will give those following your vision confidence and an avenue to be involved in the work.

Spiritual goals help us understand the will of God. When we write down our goals it becomes readily apparent whether those goals are directed by God or born out of our wishful thinking or fleshly desires. As we seek the Lord for a plan to accomplish each goal, the Spirit brings confirmation as to whether this is a goal from God or whether it is in His purpose for this particular time.

Spiritual goals help us separate our ideas from His purpose. As we commune with the Lord over our goals and plans He increasingly refines, clarifies, and defines the vision given us. In ministry there is the constant quest of separating that which is of self from that which is of the Spirit. Establishing goals clarifies and reinforces our purpose.

Spiritual goals help us know where we are in achieving our visions and completing our ministries. It is a sad commentary on much of modern church leadership that some do not know what needs to be done to complete their ministries and therefore have little idea when or if those ministries will ever be completed. If we have a vision that is from the Lord, we need understanding as to what to do to bring that vision to pass and where we are in that process. Only written goals can show us what we have accomplished and what is yet to be done. At some point in every ministry there ought to be a time when the minister can say with confidence, *"I have finished the work which Thou gavest me to do."*[9]

A Few Practical Steps in Writing Spiritual Goals

As mentioned earlier, spiritual goals must be in written form or they will, for the most part, be just wishful thinking. If you have not written down your goals, the following are a few steps you can take to establish workable, written, spiritual goals.

1. Take your written vision, break it down into its various parts, and ask God what goals need to be implemented to make those parts functional.

2. Take a notebook and list your short-term goals, those requiring six months or less, and your long-term goals, those requiring more than six months to complete. Ask the Lord for a plan to complete each. What is it that you are going to do to make these goals a reality? Your goals will form the basis for prayer related to your ministry and give those associated with you understanding of how to pray.

3. Make a daily "To Do" list. A simple "To Do" list is to take a note card and list those things related to your goals that you need to do today. List them by order of importance working from the top to the bottom. At the end of each day make your list for the following day. Include on that list any items not completed from the previous day's list. In a short time you will see the order it brings and the encouragement that comes when you see these goals being accomplished. This kind of list will help you allocate your time far more effectively.

4. Reevaluate your goals regularly. Your goals are something that can be incorporated into your daily prayer. Make it a point to take a few minutes each week to look at your listed goals and make adjustments as needed.

Of course the points above are only one method among many for establishing written goals and effectively bringing them to pass. They are only listed as one practical way to bring their effective implementation. A godly plan is essential to bring about the successful completion of ministry. The ability to establish plans and goals to achieve them are an important aid to all ministry sons.

ENDNOTES

1. Ephesians 5:17.
2. 1 Timothy 1:16.
3. Titus 2:7.
4. Philippians 3:14.
5. Deuteronomy 1:23 NKJV.
6. Luke 4:16.
7. 1 Corinthians 9:24.
8. 1 Corinthians 14:10.
9. John 17:4.

CHAPTER SEVEN

UNDERSTANDING THE BODY
IS ESSENTIAL TO ORDER

To establish father/son order requires us to see the Body of Christ in a greater dimension. Many view the Body only as an organization or the association of Christians throughout the world. Some even see it as being made up of the adherents to a particular denomination. Father/son order is about connection and relationship. To apply this order we need to understand the connection and relationship of the Body in greater ways.

Our Starting Point Is Always Found at Truth

"Truth is not a destination; truth is a highway." Many look at truth as a goal or objective rather than as the unfolding revelation of God and His creation. When a person looks at truth as a destination, he uses whatever truth he may have as a vehicle to bring judgment on those who have not arrived at the same place as he. Truth to this person becomes a point of separation rather than an instrument for understanding the riches and wonders of God.

This brings to mind the admonitions of Jesus, *"If therefore the light that is in thee be darkness, how great is that darkness."*[1] And in another place, *"For he that hath, to him shall be given: and he that hath not, from him shall be taken **even that which he hath**."*[2]

Denominational labels don't tell us what a certain church believes but rather where it stopped. Truth is an infinite road along which are billeted a multitude of treasures if we are willing and courageous enough to reach out and walk on into ever increasing heights in God.

If we are walking the highway of truth then we should not terminate our quest at markers set down by others, but instead we should use these markers to propel us into even greater understanding. If truth to us is a destination, then we are likely to separate people according to what they believe. But if it is a highway, then we will look at people according to who they are in Christ.

For the word of the Lord is right; and all His works are done in truth.[3]

Behold, thou desirest truth in the inward parts: and in the hidden part thou shalt make me to know wisdom.[4]

Jesus saith unto him, I am the way, the truth, and the life: no man cometh unto the Father, but by Me.[5]

Then said Jesus to those Jews which believed on Him, If ye continue in My word, then are ye My disciples indeed; and ye shall know the truth, and the truth shall make you free.[6]

To this end was I born, and for this cause came I into the world, that I should bear witness unto the truth. Every one that is of the truth heareth My voice. Pilate saith unto Him, What is truth?[7]

What is truth? Philosophers and sages throughout time have wrestled with this question, regularly being at odds with one another. As Paul said, many in the world are, *"Ever learning, and never able to come to the knowledge of the truth."*[8] As Christians we know that truth is related to the Word of God, *"Thy word is truth."*[9] We know that Jesus is the truth, *"I am...the truth,"*[10] and we know that Jesus is also the Word, *"The Word was made flesh."*[11]

Do we as Christians understand truth to be correct biblical teachings or do we understand it as something more? It is possible, as with Pilate, to stare truth in the face and not realize it; to try to destroy truth because of an unwillingness to receive it; to pronounce a death sentence upon truth by making it a destination rather than a highway. Like the resurrection, or the Word of God, or eternal life, truth is not an event or a religious concept, but a person, the Lord Jesus Christ. It is impossible to grow in truth without first growing in Jesus.

Unfortunately, many in Christianity have made truth the accumulation of factual knowledge rather than what it should be in our lives, which is a way of thinking. Knowing or believing things that are true does not mean that we have truth. A person who believes the earth rotates around the sun believes something that is true, but does he have truth?

A person who believes that Jesus is the Son of God, believes something that is true, but does he have truth? Many religious leaders in Jesus' day believed the Torah was God's Word. They believed Yahweh was the one true God. They believed and taught the creation and Noah's flood. They believed many true things, but they did not possess truth (see First John 2:4 and John 8:44-47).

Truth to Christians must become more than just the accumulation of accurate Bible knowledge. If we use the correct biblical facts we possess to hold others in judgment we demonstrate our lack of the truth. Improper judgment of others is the clearest sign of a failure to discern truth. If I am incapable of receiving right things from someone who is not of my denominational stripe or may not understand all that I do or challenges me to think on a higher level, I demonstrate by my improper judgment a lack of willingness to walk in truth. We are not to believe or receive everything that is spoken to us, but our attitude is a clear window to the truth we possess.

Only the most pompous and arrogant of souls would profess to understand *all* truth. It is possible to believe wrong things and still have truth; for truth is a way of thinking and not just the accumulation of accurate knowledge. Which of us has not been made aware by the Spirit of some error in our attitude, action, or belief that required change? Walking in truth, then, is walking in the thoughts of Jesus. Truth allows us to see others as He sees them, to understand God and His relationship to man as Jesus understood them. It allows us to have a life that is under the control of the Spirit rather than one under our carnal mind.

If we sought relationship over the accumulation of biblical knowledge, we would find a significant increase in the revelation of God toward us. Truth in us comes as a consequence of a growing relationship with Jesus. Truth in the Body comes as a consequence of a growing relationship with each other. When the Spirit is free to move among us and through us without the fear of criticism, judgment, or contention, the ability of the Body to receive revelation and grow in truth is multiplied.

"Behold, Thou desirest truth in the inward parts."[12] Truth in the inward or hidden parts is having our thinking transformed into true thinking. It is only in truth that the revelation and understanding of doctrine has any positive purpose. The works that Jesus would do in and through us can only be done in truth. Jesus promises us freedom in knowing the truth—not in knowing true facts, but in having a thought process that is controlled by the truth.

Hidden Truth of the Body

And He said unto them, Unto you it is given to know the mystery of the kingdom of God.[13]

Now ye are the body of Christ, and members in particular.[14]

Establishing proper father/son order unlocks hidden truths in the connection of ministry and its relationship to the Body. Mysteries in the Bible are hidden or secret truths. According to Jesus, disciples in relationship are in a position to know the mysteries of the Kingdom, a privilege that is not afforded to all (see Matt. 13:11). Hidden truths, like the fruit of most trees, lay in the higher branches of God's wisdom.

It does not require mental genius or personal perfection to attain these truths, but a right heart on a quest for order and knowledge of the Holy One. It is necessary to have a willingness and ability not to see through the distorted lens of our fears, religious beliefs, and personal experiences in order that truth (not facts, but a way of thinking) can become established in us.

There are many mysteries spoken of in the New Testament. The mystery of faith, the mystery of iniquity, the mystery of God, the mystery of the candlesticks, the mystery of Christ, the mystery of the gospel, and the mystery of Babylon are some of the mysteries to which we are called to seek understanding. They each contain hidden truths that unlock vast areas in relating to and understanding God. As we study each one in context we begin to see a unifying pattern that ties each to the others. Each mystery is in some way related to the gathering, perfection, and manifestation of the Body of Christ. An understanding of the Body of Christ, which is itself a mystery, is central in discerning the unfolding hidden truths of God's Word.

When we study the Lord's relationship to the saints and His ministry in and through them, we see a number of words that connect with each other to give enlightenment. Body, temple, house, habitation, abode, church, communion, vessel, Heaven, member, bride, and city are all words describing, in some measure, the residency of

God with us. The Body of Christ is much more than just a gathering of believers.

Not only have we not yet begun to fellowship the Body of Christ, in some ways we do not even understand what it is or how it functions. A gathering of people, a denomination of churches, or an association of believers are all referred to by some as the Body of Christ, but what really constitutes the Body of Christ? What mystery of God is revealed in and through the Body?

We Are the Temple of God

My tabernacle also shall be with them: yea, I will be their God, and they shall be My people.[15]

And I will give them an heart to know Me, that I am the Lord: and they shall be My people, and I will be their God: for they shall return unto Me with their whole heart.[16]

And I heard a great voice out of heaven saying, Behold, the tabernacle of God is with men, and He will dwell with them, and they shall be His people, and God Himself shall be with them, and be their God.[17]

And what agreement hath the temple of God with idols? for ye are the temple of the living God; as God hath said, I will dwell in them, and walk in them; and I will be their God, and they shall be My people.[18]

The order of ministry within the temple is the order of father and son. The Lord desires to not only dwell *with* us but *in* us. He has never been, as some teach, a detached God, looking on from afar. God is not like an artist who displays His many creative works for His own self-gratification. In God's eyes, mankind was not meant to be one of His many creations to be hung on the wall of His gallery of achievement. Man was created not only to worship God and to give Him glory but to be an eternal dwelling place for Him.

As the Scripture has said, *"Ye are the temple of God; ye are the body of Christ; know ye not that your bodies are the members of Christ? We have this treasure in earthen vessels; ye also are builded together for an habitation of God through the Spirit; ye also, as lively stones, are built up a spiritual house."*[19] God's will is to dwell in us and from us make an eternal habitation for His Spirit. This (not beautiful mansions in the clouds) is our heavenly destination.

When God filled us with His Spirit, it was not a completed work that He achieved: *"He which hath **begun** a good work in you will perform it until the day of Jesus Christ."*[20] He's still working in His Body to bring it to perfection. He gave us a taste of heavenly places so that we would desire to seek completion and perfection in Him: *"Ye were sealed with that Holy Spirit of promise, which is the earnest of our inheritance,"* and also: *"But I follow after, if that I may apprehend that for which also I am apprehended of Christ Jesus."*[21] The baptism of the Holy Spirit was never meant to be an end or a stopping point or a sign of our arrival but rather a beginning in the process that would lead to maturity and the completion of our purpose. We have not received our full inheritance in Him but only the down payment of a larger and greater glory and purpose to which He calls us.

The Word of God can be understood in at least three different levels or dimensions. When Jesus said, *"Destroy this temple, and in three days I will raise it up,"*[22] some who heard thought He was speaking of the natural temple. Others believe He was only speaking of His body at the resurrection. He was also giving forth a prophetic announcement of His Body, the Church, which would be raised up in the third day or the third millennium. His natural body

THE ORDER OF A Son

was taken from the earth at the resurrection. The Body that now manifests His Spirit in the earth is that of the Church.

It was Jesus' testimony of raising up this body in the third day that brought accusation from the unlearned and jealous that He was worthy of death. We are living in the third day from Jesus. It is in our day that His Body is being raised up. Jesus is the one doing it. It is not of man or from man but only by the Spirit as He teaches us to enter the Kingdom and walk in all truth. As of now, many do not yet understand what God is doing or how it will be accomplished. Like many in the days of Jesus, some think such a thing to be absurd, an impossibility only worthy of ridicule; yet God is doing exactly this with those who have eyes to see.

The Temple of the Antichrist

Many are concerned in the natural about a temple that is to be built in Israel that will house the antichrist. Many do not consider that if we are the temple of God, then the greater temple in which the antichrist spirit may reside is not one made with hands but the carnal mind of man: "*He as God sitteth in the temple of God, showing himself that he is God.*"[23] The greater rule of the antichrist is the deception that what the carnal mind thinks is God is not God at all but an antichrist spirit portraying God. As Paul said in Romans: "*The carnal mind is enmity against God: for it is not subject to the law of God, neither indeed can be.*"[24]

An illustration of this occurs in Matthew chapter 16 where Jesus has been speaking of His death, burial, and resurrection. Peter in his carnal mind is housing religious thoughts that appear so compassionate, "Let this never happen to you," but they are really thoughts of satan. Peter tells the Lord what seem to be the consoling words of a friend: "*Be it far from Thee, Lord: this shall not be unto Thee,*"[25] but satan is the one who is actually speaking from Peter's temple.

122

There may come a man, designated by some as antichrist, who will sit in a building in Jerusalem, but his power would only be temporal if he were not able to reign in the greater temple of the mind of man. Carnality affects not only the lost but also the Christian who has not come to perfection as well. This is by far the greater danger.

The spirit of antichrist has always been in the world and manifested at times through various people and rulers. *"Ye have heard that antichrist shall come, even now are there many antichrists."*[26] While many Christians are taught to look for antichrist appearing on the world's political and religious scene, dwelling in a temple in Jerusalem *"made with hands,"* most never consider his residence in the greater *"house made without hands"* that displays this spirit through its carnality.[27]

Can a Christian be affected by carnality? Wasn't carnality done away with at the time of our initial salvation? Listen to the apostle Paul as he speaks to Christians in several of his writings: *"Are ye not carnal; but I am carnal, sold under sin; I, brethren, could not speak unto you as unto spiritual, but as unto carnal; for ye are yet carnal; are ye not carnal, and walk as men?"*[28] There is a death to the carnal mind that is required for saints and the Church to come into perfection or maturity. Father/son order is an order of relationship. This order will bring maturity to the Church.

Much of what is spoken of as the power of the Spirit in modern Christianity is nothing more than attempts by Christians to demonstrate the Spirit while walking in the carnality of their mind. While professing liberty and truth, many are really bound by fears, traditions, desires for material prosperity and elevated positions of honor. Antichrist *"sitteth [resides and rules] in the temple of God, showing himself that he is God."*[29]

Each of us, as Christians, need to be more concerned about the intrusion of an antichrist spirit in our temple and in the Church, which is the Body of Christ, than we do about a brick and mortar temple in the land of Israel. *"What? know ye not that your body is the temple of the Holy Ghost."*[30] Unfortunately many do not recognize the greater mystery and the greater temple of God. Remember, the natural world reveals what is already happening in the spiritual realm. The natural helps us understand the spiritual; the natural is not greater and it does not control the spiritual.

Signs represented by earthquakes and floods, our present fatherless generation, propagation of homosexual lifestyles, and many others are really signs that speak more of a weak and anemic, rudderless Church than they do of a debased world. The natural world is only making visible the spiritual state of the Church. If we truly want to change the world, we as Christians need to allow the Lord to change His Church into His image. Father/son order will help all in the Church bring about this change into His image.

Assembling the Body

Not forsaking the assembling of ourselves together, as the manner of some is; but exhorting one another: and so much the more, as ye see the day approaching.[31]

Father/son order is the order of ministry in the Kingdom. Ministry, in part, has the responsibility of fostering the assemblage of the Body. The Church is the Body of Christ, but it is not yet the perfected, manifested Body of Christ. *"Beloved, now are we the sons of God, and it **doth not yet appear** what we shall be."*[32] As the Kingdom is present within us but has not yet been manifested in the world, so in some ways is the Church.

The Church is yet to be perfected. *"That **He might present it** to Himself a glorious church, not having spot, or wrinkle, or any such thing; but that it should be holy and without blemish."*[33] There is a great mystery of Christ and His Church that is unfolding in our day. *"This is a great mystery: but I speak concerning Christ and* *the church.*"[34] Many in our day are coming to understand in greater measure what the true Body of Christ is and its purpose in completing the will and prophecy of God.

Paul admonishes us not to forsake the *"assembling of ourselves together."*[35] On one level of understanding, many interpret this to mean that we need to be in church services when they are scheduled. This may generally be true, but if we allow the Lord to stretch us and to lay hold of a higher realm of truth, we would see that the assembling together is a process that requires order, change, and growth. The word *assemble* means to fit together in one the various parts. It reminds us of Paul's instruction to the Ephesians to be *"fitly joined together and compacted by that which every joint supplieth, according to the effectual working in the measure of every part, maketh increase of the body unto the edifying of itself in love."*[36]

Assembling ourselves together, then, becomes the process by which we as individual members of Christ's Body become joined through the Spirit into a Body that is increasing toward perfection. A local church can have all its membership attend church at the same time and not be assembled together. Just being in the same building does not bring forth an assembling, but being of the same mind and vision does: *"That ye be perfectly joined together in the same mind and in the same judgment."*[37]

Paul tells us that the manner of some is to forsake this assembling together. As our spiritual eyes are enlightened to see the unfolding plan of God in our day we need to work toward a unity and relationship that will bring forth the manifestation of the Body; so much the more, as we see the day approaching. To be assembled together is going to involve much more than just meeting together in the same building once or twice a week.

This assembling is going to require that we first have a true vision; second, that the church seek, understand, and follow that vision; third, that the members of the Body seek, understand, and follow right biblical order. After these, the church must understand and practice the doctrine, see their individual places in the Body, come forth in their particular ministries, and complete the various other functions designated for the Body. The Body must begin to love itself for it is the Body of Christ. In this way the Body can be *"of the same mind and in the same judgment; fitly joined together and compacted by that which every joint supplieth."*[38] This is a process, and it must be ruled by the Spirit.

Remembering the Body of Christ

So we, being many, are one body in Christ, and every one members one of another.[39]

For as the body is one, and hath many members, and all the members of that one body, being many, are one body: so also is Christ...Now ye are the body of Christ, and members in particular.[40]

The cup of blessing which we bless, is it not the communion of the blood of Christ? The bread which we break, is it not the communion of the body of Christ?[41]

And He took bread, and gave thanks, and brake it, and gave unto them, saying, This is My body which is given for you: this do in remembrance of Me.[42]

Father/son relationship is a connection according to the will of the Holy Spirit. The assembling of the Body of Christ is the connecting of its various parts into one Body. Each saint is a member and all the members being properly joined together form one Body. The function of this Body is local in nature.

And when they had ordained them elders in every church.... Unto the church of God which is at Corinth....

And at that time there was a great persecution against the church which was at Jerusalem.... And when he had landed at Caesarea, and gone up, and saluted the church.... He sent to Ephesus, and called the elders of the church.... A servant of the church which is at Cenchrea.... Likewise greet the church that is in their house.[43]

The apostle Paul's approach to the Church was according to location. He ordained elders in every city. He sent ministry sons to various locations to deal with the church on a local and personal level. Each local church had autonomy and was not controlled by a headquarters but by elders taken from among the saints.

For this cause have I sent unto you Timotheus, who is my beloved son, and faithful in the Lord, who shall bring you into remembrance of my ways which be in Christ, as I teach every where in every church.[44]

What is the great mystery of this Body, the Church that resides in various locations throughout the earth? Jesus presented the most powerful truth about this mystery at the Last Supper. For over three years He had been ministering to His disciples about the Kingdom of God. He spoke to them at various times of His death, burial, and resurrection that needed to be accomplished. Understanding His death, burial, and resurrection is the framework for understanding the gospel.

Moreover, brethren, I declare unto you the gospel which I preached unto you, which also ye have received, and wherein ye stand...For I delivered unto you first of all that which I also received, how that Christ died for our sins according to the scriptures; and that He was buried, and that He rose again the third day according to the scriptures.[45]

Before He goes to His death and rises again, He eats one last meal with the Twelve. It was not natural food but the Word of God in flesh that gave the disciples their real food. One last time they would have an opportunity to "partake of His flesh" in its present form, before a new order of communing with Jesus would be established. On this final opportunity to minister from the Word of God, Jesus took this occasion to instruct His disciples about the Body of Christ. He desired to have this final meal with them, in part, because it would become a pattern for Christians in assembling His Body. Jesus, in John chapter 6, explains this part of the mystery that is still hidden from most of the church world.

> *I am that bread of life. Your fathers did eat manna in the wilderness, and are dead. This is the bread which cometh down from heaven, that a man may eat thereof, and not die. I am the living bread which came down from heaven: if any man eat of this bread, he shall live for ever: and the bread that I will give is My flesh, which I will give for the life of the world.... Then Jesus said unto them, Verily, verily, I say unto you, Except ye eat the flesh of the Son of man, and drink His blood, ye have no life in you.... As the living Father hath sent Me, and I live by the Father: so he that eateth Me, even he shall live by Me.... Not as your fathers did eat manna, and are dead: he that eateth of this bread shall live for ever.... The Jews then murmured at Him, because He said, I am the bread which came down from heaven.... The Jews therefore strove among themselves, saying, How can this man give us His flesh to eat? Then Jesus said unto them, Verily, verily, I*

say unto you, Except ye eat the flesh of the Son of man, and drink His blood, ye have no life in you.[46]

Christians have understood this portion of Scripture in numerous ways. Some believe Jesus was speaking figuratively by saying that Christians must identify with His life and sacrifice. Others believe He was teaching that we must literally eat His flesh through a "divine" process of transubstantiation. All hold these words to be important, but vary greatly in their understanding. Jesus tells us we must eat His flesh and that eating His flesh brings life; in fact, if we don't eat His flesh we have no life in us. From His words it's easy to see how some even believe that partaking of communion is necessary for salvation.

The flesh of Jesus that housed the Word was about to go to its death. He told the disciples it was for their benefit that He would be leaving: "*Nevertheless I tell you the truth; it is expedient for you that I go away: for if I go not away, the Comforter will not come unto you; but if I depart, I will send Him unto you.*"[47] Something greater was going to take the place of His flesh that was about to leave the earth.

He was leaving the earth in the fleshly form of His body but He would be returning in His Spirit: "*And I will pray the Father, and He shall give you another Comforter, that He may abide with you for ever; even the Spirit of truth; whom the world cannot receive, because it seeth Him not, neither knoweth Him: but ye know Him; for He dwelleth with you, and shall be in you. I will not leave you comfortless: I will come to you.*"[48] The great mystery of His Body, the Church, was unfolding. Jesus would be here on earth with us but not in the body of His flesh, but in His Body, the Church.

It would be a Body that would be able to have a greater effect on the world. Jesus, not just in one body of flesh, but in the many membered Body of the Church. The world has yet to see this Body in its perfection. Jesus promised that if He would be lifted up—if His church would ever get into the place where what it was manifesting was only Jesus and not its own flesh and disorder—then He would draw all men unto Him.

The world does not see Jesus in the Church. It sees division, self-seeking, competition, jealousy, successful business practices, but it doesn't as yet see Jesus. This is all changing. As the Church grasps its real purpose and identity and seeks perfection rather than escape or material success, the Lord Jesus will become clearer to all who look upon His Body. All who look upon His Body will begin to see the great God of the universe, a God of power and love.

All doctrines that connect us in relationship (such as marriage, baptism, communion, tithing, repentance, etc.) have a natural sign as a component of that doctrine. They each involve some act that we do in the earth that in the Spirit provides for us a heavenly connection. This is what Jesus did for us when He instituted communion at the Last Supper. The natural sign or act that we are told to do is the partaking of bread (His body) and wine (the blood covenant).

It is clear from our traditions that many Christians do not understand what they are really doing when partaking of communion. Some believe they are actually eating the literal flesh and blood of Jesus. Many believe it to be a memorial of His death from First Corinthians chapter 11. When we participate in communion, we are not eating the literal flesh and blood of Jesus. Nor is communion simply for us to remember the sacrifice of Jesus given for us.

What Christian is there who does not know that Jesus died for us? The Church is not in danger of forgetting Jesus' death. It does not require periodic participation in communion to reflect on that event to keep it alive in the minds of the saints. These are religious concepts that for the most part are born out of tradition, not spiritual concepts that come forth from the Word. The Church is in danger, and indeed, in large part has neglected to manifest Jesus' Body.

When Jesus sat before His disciples He took bread, blessed it, and broke it into pieces and gave it to each disciple. He said, *"This is My body...this do in remembrance of Me."* The bread illustrated His body that was to be given on the cross for them. Each disciple now possessed a piece of the bread of His body. What were they supposed to do with it? Take it and eat it and do this in remembrance of Jesus. The pieces of bread were all parts of the one body from which they came. We are told by Paul, *"Ye are the body of Christ and members in particular."*[49] We are the pieces that make up the Body of Christ. What are the *members* of His Body supposed to do? Re*member* Jesus. Re-member—meaning to member again.

Remembering can mean bringing thoughts back into our conscious mind—which is how it is most often understood. It can also mean to bring back into physical being, as in the assembling of parts of a puzzle into the whole. When Jesus asks us to do this in *"remembrance of Me,"*[50] He is telling His followers, "Put My body back together again!" "My body, which is broken for you, must now be remembered—the members have to be put together again—in the Body of My Church!"

The thief on the cross asked Jesus, *"**Remember me** when Thou comest into Thy kingdom."*[51] He isn't just asking Jesus to think about him and the time they had together at Calvary. No, he wants Jesus to take him with Him to His kingdom. He wants to literally come into existence in God's Kingdom, not just to be a thought in Jesus' mind. This Jesus promised to do for Him. This is how he was remembered.

When we partake of communion, it is this process that we are to facilitate. Communion ought to be a time of coming into union with one another—comm*union*—literally meaning, "with union."

It was originally celebrated as part of a meal along with the fellowship of the saints. The passing out of wafers and little plastic cups full of grape juice was a later, religious development. The Last Supper of Jesus, this last meal that in His words, *"with desire I have desired to eat this passover with you before I suffer,"*[52] was of such longing for Jesus because it would establish the framework for the manifestation of His Body in the Church.

> *For I have received of the Lord that which also I delivered unto you, That the Lord Jesus the same night in which He was betrayed took bread: And when He had given thanks, He brake it, and said, Take, eat: this is My body, which is broken for you: this do in remembrance of Me. After the same manner also He took the cup, when He had supped, saying, This cup is the new testament in My blood: this do ye, as oft as ye drink it, in remembrance of Me. For as often as ye eat this bread, and drink this cup, ye do show the Lord's death till He come. Wherefore whosoever shall eat this bread, and drink this cup of the Lord, unworthily, shall be guilty of the body and blood of the Lord. But let a man examine himself, and so let him eat of that bread, and drink of that cup. For he that eateth and drinketh unworthily, eateth and drinketh damnation to himself, not discerning the Lord's body. For this cause many are weak and sickly among you, and many sleep. For if we would judge ourselves, we should not be judged. But when we are judged, we are chastened of the Lord, that we should not be condemned with the world. Wherefore, my brethren, when ye come together to eat, tarry one for another.*[53]

This was the instruction given Paul by the Lord. We are to partake of communion until He comes. Until the Lord is manifested in

His Body, the Church, we are to be about the process of remembering ourselves into one unified Body. Whoever eats and drinks this meal unworthily (that is to treat it as a common or ordinary meal) is *"guilty of the body and blood of the Lord."* Why? Because they work against the assembling of the Body. For this reason some are weak and sick and some have even died. Not that God is punishing them because they didn't pray long enough before they took communion or because they shared a laugh with someone and did not show "proper reverence" when they ate the bread.

No, some are weak and sick and some have even died because, like so many they don't recognize and understand one another as members of the Body of Christ. Some member could have ministered healing; some member of the Body could have supplied the strength that was lacking; some member had God's answer to an overwhelming need, but it could not be received because they didn't discern what the true Body of Christ is. Some show their disdain for the Body by holding it or some of its members in disdain.

They judge the Body so they are unable to receive from it. Or they separate themselves from the Body. "We hear God. God ministers through us. We can have God without having relationship with a Church." They separate themselves from the Body and the government of God and suffer the consequences usually without ever understanding why. These are those which have desire for association but not for relationship.

As we understand what the Lord is doing in our day and how He is going to return, then the importance of the Body and our need to allow the Spirit to bring about its unity and perfection takes on increased significance. In the fellowship of taking communion, we then ask ourselves questions such as, What is my part in the Body? To whom am joined, how and for what purpose? How can I better manifest Christ? How can I better bring about the order of God through submission and service? How can I help the

Church and its leadership to fulfill the vision for the Church given by God?

A Prayer for Understanding the Body

We pray for the Body that it might become one, that it might manifest Jesus to the world, that it might grow in unity, understanding, and love.

We pray for the individual members of the Body for our perfection is dependent upon them and theirs upon us. We increasingly see Jesus in our brothers and sisters. There is a growing desire to protect and nurture the Body. We come to understand that the salvation of the world and the fulfillment of the Lord's promises to us are dependent upon this Body of which we are a part.

We desire the health of the Body. We become more careful not to speak ill of the Body or bring harm to the Body by careless actions or speech. These and like considerations now form the basis for our participation in communion. Communion to us now becomes more than just the occasional eating of bread and grape juice but part of an ongoing spiritual exercise to bring forth the completed, perfected, mature Body of Christ which is the Church.

The Many Membered Body of Christ

I beseech you therefore, brethren, by the mercies of God, that ye present your bodies a living sacrifice, holy, acceptable unto God, which is your reasonable service.... For as we have many members in one body, and all members have not the same office: So we, being many, are one body in Christ, and every one members one of another.[54]

For as the body is one, and hath many members, and all the members of that one body, being many, are one body: so also is Christ.... But now hath God set the members every one of them in the body, as it hath pleased Him. And if they were all one member, where were the body? But now are they many members, yet but one body.[55]

For the earnest expectation of the creature waiteth for the manifestation of the sons of God.[56]

Father/son order brings us back to the original biblical order destroyed by sin. The Bible tells us that with the fall of man not only did sin cause humankind to dwell under a curse but all of creation as well. The natural world was cursed for the benefit of man. Since that time *"the whole creation groans and labors with birth pangs together until now."*[57]

Why is it groaning and travailing? Because it is waiting for a redemption that will restore it to its pre-cursed state. Not only creation but the elect as well have this understanding and longing: *"And not only they, but ourselves also, which have the firstfruits of the Spirit, even we ourselves groan within ourselves, waiting for the adoption, to wit, the redemption of our body."*[58]

Earthquakes, pestilence, and the like are the travail of the earth waiting for an event that will reorder the universe. When will this happen? When the sons of God who are as yet hidden, become revealed. What will start this revealing? When the Church, which is the Body of Christ, is perfected to reveal Jesus to the world. Who makes up this Body? The members of this Body are God's elect who have heard His call to order. How have they heard this call? They have witnessed the spirit of Elijah turning the hearts of the fathers to sons and the hearts of sons to fathers. What is their goal? Their goal is not human perfection but relationship with the Lord and each other and the manifestation of Jesus in His Body.

This Body of Christ is a many membered Body. In times past great men and women of God have arisen, bringing forth great moves of God, particular revelations, or unique and gifted ministries. As great as they may have been, none of them were ever able to complete the plan of God for the world. In this last day it is not an exalted ministry but a manifested Body that shall restore a truth and a power far in excess of anything seen heretofore.

The Word tells us that what will be unique about this Body is that it will not be individual members which are exalted, but the Lord Jesus. It is Jesus who is and will be seen as the head of this Body. Creation is waiting for this to happen and so are the saints who have gone on before us.

> *God having provided some better thing for us, that they without us should not be made perfect.*[59]

> *And they cried with a loud voice, saying, How long, O Lord, holy and true, dost Thou not judge and avenge our blood on them that dwell on the earth? ...for a little season, until their fellowservants also and their brethren, that should be killed as they were, should be fulfilled.*[60]

We have to learn to look at the work the Lord has given us to do in the context of the Body of Christ. We need to look at ourselves not as independent workers for God's kingdom, but as particular members of this Body. When we view ourselves as independent workers, then all ministry and all that God is doing in the earth revolves around us. When we look at ourselves as one of many members of a Body, then what God is doing is conditioned upon my relationship with the other members and the perfection of that Body. The Church has not yet seen itself in this light.

Most saints seek a calling from God and see that calling independent from the Body. If they do not understand the biblical concept of father/son order, Body relationships will suffer. Due to a lack of maturity and understanding, many feel if they have a call from God they have a sanction to cut ties with one group and seek association with another. This attitude comes from the disorder wrought out of patterning the Church after the order of men and not the order of God.

The Body to many is equated with the particular church they attend. They attend in order to worship, hear preaching, receive teaching, or to have a place in which they can perform some function related to ministry. It is viewed much as a club or organization that we can join rather than a living, spiritual entity into which we are born by the will of God.

If it is something I choose to join, then I can also choose to disassociate myself with it and search for another "club" more to my liking. If, however, it is a living Body into which I am placed by God, then it's not a matter of my personal choice. My spiritual life, and to some degree the life of those I am in relationship with, is dependent upon maintaining the proper God ordained order of the Body. Numerous churches today are, in truth, little more than religious orphanages. Many who attend these "orphanages," however, and many who have stopped attending these substitutes for Christ's Body, are hungering for relationship with the true Body of Christ. This is a hunger the Lord is bringing and it is a hunger that He will satisfy as His Body the Church is made manifest.

When we were saved, one of the obligations and one of the privileges of that salvation was our relationship with the Body of Christ. Just having a right does not necessarily mean we are functioning in that Body according to the will of Him who called us. There is abundant scriptural direction as to how we are to function in the Body and the dangers of not properly relating to the Body or disassociating ourselves from the Body. One of the revelations being brought forth by the Spirit in our day is an understanding of the true Body of Christ, its operation and its government.

We may have the baptism of the Holy Spirit, and access to the Body but have we allowed that Spirit to establish us in relationship with His true Body? Saints of like spirit, who are being led by the Spirit, are being called into relationship out of church systems developed by man and into a Body ordained by God. God's church today is in this transition.

> *For by one Spirit are we all baptized into one body, whether we be Jews or Gentiles, whether we be bond or free; and have been all made to drink into one Spirit.*[61]

We see ourselves in our personal relationship with God, but many have difficulty in seeing their ministry as only a member or portion of a much greater ministry. If we saw ourselves this way, our personal agendas would take back seat to the greater purposes of God. We would begin to think generationally and seek ministry order. We would not be trying to exalt self but Jesus in the Body. Pride for all that we accomplish would disappear when it is apparent that all that is done, is done by the hand of Jesus through a many membered Body.

To walk in this type of relationship with the Body is going to require the death of a lot of flesh. Yet this is exactly the Body for which Jesus is coming and in which He will appear. Not an anemic and self-centered church but a *"glorious church, not having spot, or wrinkle, or any such thing; but that it should be holy and without blemish."*[62]

This can only happen as we are obedient to present our *"bodies a living sacrifice, holy, acceptable unto God, which is your reasonable service."*[63] Our agendas die as our identities and ministries become entwined with His true Body and our desire to see Jesus increasingly displayed through that Body.

Related Scriptures

The following are groupings of various Scriptures related to the topic of the Body of Christ and descriptions of these verses as they pertain to this topic.

The Body as the Man of God

All scripture is given by inspiration of God, and is profitable for doctrine, for reproof, for correction, for instruction in righteousness: That the man of God may be perfect, thoroughly furnished unto all good works.[64]

Till we all come in the unity of the faith, and of the knowledge of the Son of God, unto a perfect man, unto the measure of the stature of the fulness of Christ.[65]

He that overcometh shall inherit all things; and I will be his God, and he shall be my son.[66]

When He shall come to be glorified in His saints, and to be admired in all them that believe (because our testimony among you was believed) in that day.[67]

So all the generations from Abraham to David are fourteen generations; and from David until the carrying away into Babylon are fourteen generations; and from the carrying away into Babylon unto Christ are fourteen generations.[68]

In His humiliation His judgment was taken away: and who shall declare His generation? for His life is taken from the earth.[69]

Father/son order is a type of the relationship of God with the corporate man. Our Father desires relationship with His sons. The appearing or revealing of Jesus will first come as Jesus is glorified in His saints, the Body of Christ. In chapter one of Matthew are listed the generations of promise. When studying the list we find that Jesus is listed as the thirteenth generation from Babylon, the fourteenth being Christ.

Who is this Christ or anointed one? This Christ is not Jesus but the generation of Jesus. It is this generation made up of saints or those who are overcomers who become the perfected Body of Christ. They make up what Jesus called, *my son*, in Revelations chapter 21. We cannot come to *"the measure of the stature of the fullness of Christ,"* until the Church becomes *a perfect man*—a Body that is mature and in ministry order and proper relationship.

The Body of Christ as Seen in the Husband and Wife Relationship

> *For the husband is head of the wife, as also Christ is head of the Church and He is the Savior of the body....Husbands love your wives just as Christ also loved the church and gave Himself for her....So husbands ought to love their own wives as their own bodies; he who loves his wife loves himself. ...This is a great mystery: but I speak concerning Christ and the church.*[70]

> *Therefore shall a man leave his father and his mother, and shall cleave unto his wife: and they shall be one flesh.*[71]

> *To the intent that now unto the principalities and powers in heavenly places might be known by the church the manifold wisdom of God.*[72]

> *According to my earnest expectation and my hope, that in nothing I shall be ashamed, but that with all boldness, as always, so now also Christ shall be magnified in my body, whether it be by life, or by death.*[73]

The Church requires change to bring perfection. God cares for us more than we care for our own flesh. The mystery of the

Church is as the relationship of husband and wife. The Church is the Body of Christ. The Church is also equated with a bride or wife. How it can be both is summed up in the mystery revealed by the phrase, *"and they shall be one flesh."*

Jesus loves His Body, the Church, and desires to be one flesh with it. Paul calls this relationship of Christ with the Church *"a great mystery."* Jesus loves the Church as His own Body, which indeed it is. From the Church the Father will receive glory and by the Church show forth His wisdom that incorporates His Body, the Church, into His plan for the restoration of all things. Our pursuit then should be to magnify Jesus in our bodies, which are to be individual members of His Body.

Jesus Is Head of the Body and Builder of the Church

> *And hath put all things under His feet, and gave Him to be the head over all things to the church.*[74]

> *And I say also unto thee, That thou art Peter, and upon this rock I will build My church; and the gates of hell shall not prevail against it.*[75]

> *Praising God, and having favour with all the people. And the Lord added to the church daily such as should be saved.*[76]

> *Which are a shadow of things to come; but the body is of Christ.*[77]

The only way that Jesus can truly be the head is if He is given preeminence in the Church. The world must see Him, not dynamic ministries or gifted individuals, as the source of all that is being accomplished by God in the Church. All glory, honor, and praise belong to Him alone: *"My glory will I not give to another."*[78] It is the head that houses wisdom. It is the head that possesses knowledge. It is the head that gives direction to the Body. The purpose of the Body is to serve the head and fulfill its desires.

Jesus is the Savior of the Body. We are privileged to be able to participate in God's plan of restoration and salvation but it is Jesus who reaches and saves the lost. We don't build the Church; Jesus does. We don't add people to the Church; once again it is the Lord's work and He does it daily, without fail. When He's building the Church, He's building His Body.

The Church Is Ruled as a Family

For this cause I bow my knees unto the Father of our Lord Jesus Christ, of whom the whole family in heaven and earth is named.[79]

But if I tarry long, that thou mayest know how thou oughtest to behave thyself in the house of God, which is the church of the living God, the pillar and ground of the truth.[80]

For if a man know not how to rule his own house, how shall he take care of the church of God.[81]

Wherefore when He cometh into the world, He saith, Sacrifice and offering thou wouldest not, but a body hast thou prepared Me.[82]

The relationship of the Church to Jesus is like that of a husband and wife. The rule of this many membered Body is like that of a family. It is not Bible school, or psychology, or ministerial gifting that equip us for rule in the Body but our understanding and ability to function as a family in godly order. Rule should not be given in the Body on the basis of having achieved a certain educational level or as a result of demonstrated gifting or even because of an ability to preach.

Rule is given by God and should be governed through leadership on the basis of understanding proper church order and being able to establish that order as would be done in a family. By equating the Body with a family, the Lord is showing us our relationship is to be according to the closest of all interpersonal relationships.

The Father wants a family. He is the Father of His family, the family of God. Our journey to come into father/son order helps establish this family. Each son of God is on a trek (Son-trek) or journey to allow the Spirit to place him in the order of God. This journey will take us from the confusion of defective systems built on broken relationships to the order of the family of God.

ENDNOTES

1. Matthew 6:23.
2. Mark 4:25.
3. Psalm 33:4.
4. Psalm 51:6.
5. John 14:6.
6. John 8:31-32.
7. John 18:37-38.
8. 2 Timothy 3:7.
9. John 17:17.
10. John 14:6.
11. John 1:14.
12. Psalm 51:6.
13. Mark 4:11.
14. 1 Corinthians 12:27.
15. Ezekiel 37:27.
16. Jeremiah 24:7.
17. Revelation 21:3.

18. 2 Corinthians 6:16.
19. 1 Corinthians 3:16; 12:27; 6:15; 2 Corinthians 4:7; Ephesians 2:22; 1 Peter 2:5.
20. Philippians 1:6.
21. Ephesians 1:13; Philippians 3:12.
22. John 2:9.
23. 2 Thessalonians 2:4.
24. Romans 8:7.
25. Matthew 16:22.
26. 1 John 2:18.
27. 2 Corinthians 5:1.
28. 1 Corinthians 3:3; Romans 7:14; 1 Corinthians 3:1,3.
29. 2 Thessalonians 2:4.
30. 1 Corinthians 6:19.
31. Hebrews 10:25.
32. 1 John 3:2.
33. Ephesians 5:27.
34. Ephesians 5:32.
35. Hebrews 10:25.
36. Ephesians 4:16.
37. 1 Corinthians 1:10.
38. 1 Corinthians 1:10; Ephesians 4:16.
39. Romans 12:5.
40. 1 Corinthians 12:12,17.
41. 1 Corinthians 10:16.
42. Luke 22:19.
43. Acts 14:23; 1 Corinthians 1:2; Acts 8:1; 18:22; 20:17; Romans 16:1,5.
44. 1 Corinthians 4:17.
45. 1 Corinthians 15:1,3-4.
46. John 6:48-51,53,57-58,41,52-53.
47. John 16:7.
48. John 14:16-18.
49. 1 Corinthians 12:27.

50. 1 Corinthians 11:24.
51. Luke 23:42.
52. Luke 22:15.
53. 1 Corinthians 11:23-33.
54. Romans 12:1,4-5.
55. 1 Corinthians 12:12,18-20.
56. Romans 8:19.
57. Romans 8:22 NKJV.
58. Romans 8:23 NKJV.
59. Hebrews 11:40.
60. Revelation 6:10-11.
61. 1 Corinthians 12:13.
62. Ephesians 5:27.
63. Romans 12:1.
64. 2 Timothy 3:16-17.
65. Ephesians 4:13.
66. Revelation 21:7.
67. 2 Thessalonians 1:10.
68. Matthew 1:17.
69. Acts 8:33.
70. Ephesians 5:23,25,28,32 NKJV.
71. Genesis 2:24.
72. Ephesians 3:10.
73. Philippians 1:20.
74. Ephesians 1:22.
75. Matthew 16:18.
76. Acts 2:47.
77. Colossians 2:17.
78. Isaiah 42:8.
79. Ephesians 3:14-15.
80. 1 Timothy 3:15.
81. 1 Timothy 3:5.
82. Hebrews 10:5.

CHAPTER EIGHT

INSIGHTS ON *YOU HAVE NOT MANY FATHERS*

The book, *You Have Not Many Fathers*, has grasped a panoramic vision of ministry order throughout Scripture. It has brought light to one of those heretofore hidden links of Scripture that connect and empower God's people through reestablishing the pattern for Bible ministry and Kingdom order. It is a great source of revelation for all seeking identity, inheritance and the completion of the Lord's purpose in their ministries. More than information, it is a textbook into the introduction of father/son order that should be assimilated into our ministries and churches.

In this chapter we will be offering insights concerning the above book. We will be looking at lessons learned and specific applications we can glean for our individual ministries. Under the heading of "Ministry Checklist" will be listed numerous questions a father can use to gauge progress in achieving this order. These questions are to serve as a type of checklist to measure our understanding and implementation of *You Have Not Many Fathers*.

Five Things That Only a Father in Ministry Can Give a Son

In reading *You Have Not Many Fathers*, it becomes apparent that there are five things that only a father in ministry can give to a son. Identity, purpose, vision, inheritance, and a father's blessing can only come in their fullness via this order. If a saint is not prepared to become a son, he will miss out on the five areas necessary to complete his or her ministry.

Identity: Fathers are a source of identity for sons. True identity does not come from church organizations, gifting, doctrine, or group affiliations. We should be Christians, but that is not our identity. Unfortunately most in Christianity do not understand who they really are in Christ. Our identity, in part, comes from understanding those things that God has placed in us that make us unique and speak of His individual creation within each human being. To understand this identity requires order and relationship.

Purpose: We as Christians should be involved in the process that brings salvation to the lost. We are to be vessels to bring light into dark places and the gospel to those in need. Saving the lost, however, is not our purpose; it's the result of a right lifestyle in proper order. God has given each saint a specific purpose. Many Christians "die with the music still in them" because they never find their true purpose in God. Without a father in ministry we will never complete our full purpose.

Vision: Vision is not just a set of goals or things that we feel the Lord has asked us to do. As described in Chapter Four, it goes far beyond this kind of understanding. God gives us vision. Vision allows us to see into the heavens concerning our ministries. It sets definition to our ministry and an understanding around which others can be gathered. Like a telescope it expands, one section being linked to the next. Without a father's vision, we have only dreams and expectations and words of knowledge. Only through a father can the clear path of vision be opened up to us.

Inheritance: By becoming Christians we have inherited salvation and many things that accompany this great gift. In ministry there is an inheritance that can only come through father/son relationship. Part of this inheritance involves a double portion that comes as a result of this relationship.

Blessing: A blessing is the act of declaring God's favor or excellence upon others. We of course are all richly blessed being Christians. The blessing from fathers to sons is a blessing in ministry. A blessing is not just spoken words for divine approval but the power of those words to bring it to pass. A blessing is like the inheritance and is, in many ways, even more important. Inheritance is the bestowing of that which is prepared and comes down to the son from the past preparation of the father. Blessing is that which speaks to our future. In the Scripture, the head of a family, prior to his death, would often make a blessing upon the next generation. This serves as a type of the father/son blessing. Without being sons in right order we will walk in ministry never being empowered by our father's blessing.

Lessons to Be Learned From Father/Son Order

Lesson One: The Church Needs Fathers

> *And I will give children to be their princes, and babes shall rule over them. And the people shall be oppressed, every one by another, and every one by his neighbor: the child shall behave himself proudly against the ancient, and the base against the honorable.*[1]

> *For though ye have ten thousand instructors in Christ, yet have ye not many fathers: for in Christ Jesus I have begotten you through the gospel.*[2]

The Church today, as the Corinthian Church of 2,000 years ago, is out of order. The reason that church was out of order is because they sought their identity from their favorite ministry or by their gifting. The answer now, as it was then, is for the Church to come into father/son order. If a church fails to do this, the people will have disorder and continued lack of identity.

Ministry Checklist

- Am I a ministry father or a boy leader?
- Is my church ordered after father/son relationship?
- Is my right to ministry based on any of the following? If so, what changes need to be made?
- A voting process of majority rule.
- Authority from headquarters.
- Men who are not in proper father/son order.
- The dictates of men over the will of God.
- My gifting or abilities.
- A Church board.
- What judgment has my ministry experienced for not following proper order in the past?
- Is my Church producing boy leaders or fathers?
- Have I established a plan to bring forth this order?
- Has the generational order of my son's sons been revealed to me?

Lesson Two: The Father's Order Must Be Established

And I will raise me up a faithful priest, that shall do according to that which is in mine heart and in my mind: and I will build him a sure house; and he shall walk before mine anointed for ever.[3]

The order of the universe became chaos when Adam decided to violate his Father's order and partook of the fruit of the knowledge of good and evil. Its fruit would be the exact opposite of the fruit of the Spirit, which would produce life. Following Adam's fall we have a succession of men and nations in which God desired to reestablish His order. Events in the lives of Cain, Abel, Seth, Noah, the Patriarchs, Moses, Joshua, Aaron and his sons, Samuel, Eli, the Kings of Israel, and others speak continually of God's desire to establish proper father/son order. To undo the disorder of God's son Adam, we must be established in the order or generation of Jesus.

Ministry Checklist

- Have I successfully taught the many patterns of father/son order given in the Bible?
- Father/son patterns of order as well as disorder are listed in the Bible. Do my sons understand the consequences of each?
- Do I understand what it is to build the house of God on the pattern of David? Do I see how this is conditioned upon proper father/son order?
- Do we as David desire to build a house for God?
- Did God want David to build Him a house?
- Does He want us to build Him a house?
- Who was to build the house for David?
- Who might want to build the house in our ministries?
- Am I able to pass on double portions to my sons?
- If my ministry were completed today, what is it that I would be passing on to my sons? Would my vision be carried on in them?
- What is it we impart to our sons through the laying on of hands?

Lesson Three: We Need to Pass On
Inheritance Through the Generations

And the Lord thy God will bring thee into the land which thy fathers possessed, and thou shalt possess it; and He will do thee good, and multiply thee above thy fathers.[4]

God desires to bring restoration to the Church. The things of righteous fathers must become the possessions of sons. God is promising in our day to not only give us the spiritual land possessed by earlier church fathers but to multiply our spiritual empowerment. The passing on of biblical inheritance from fathers to sons is the method to bring this to pass.

Ministry Checklist

- As a ministry father, can I put down on paper the inheritance I am passing on to ministry sons?
- Are my ministry sons in position to receive inheritance?
- Am I in a position to receive inheritance from my father in ministry?
- Have the generations of my sons been ordered?
- What will happen to my ministry if my sons are not in set in order?
- How will I know if the generations are ordered properly?
- Has my understanding of "end time" events hindered the desire or ability to order my generations or pass on inheritance?
- Has an "any second now" mentality been keeping my sons' and my eyes off the greater work the Lord would have done?
- Is this mentality keeping me from seeing His many comings and goings in Scripture and in daily life?
- By so limiting my focus, has it placed a hold on establishing inheritance or generations?
- Has it hindered our understanding or ability to come up, go up, rise up, or experience the revealing or appearing of the Lord?
- Do my ministry sons respect and seek after legitimacy and inheritance?

Lesson Four: Set Ministry Needs a Father's Heart

And it was in the heart of David my father to build an house for the name of the Lord God of Israel. And the Lord said unto David my father, Whereas it was in thine heart to build an house unto My name, thou didst well that it was in thine heart.[5]

The heart of a ministry father needs to be toward allowing God to fulfill his purpose and plan in ministry. God has it all figured out and knows exactly how to do it. The heart of a true father is toward his son and his son's welfare—to empower the son so that he may excel and receive inheritance. Like Jesus, his heart is controlled not by those things of the present but by what his ministry will manifest in the earth in following generations. A heart that is focused properly allows the Lord to bring forth a progressive work in ministry.

Ministry Checklist

- Is my heart the heart of a father or some other kind?
- What is the heart of a hireling?
- What is the heart of an adolescent?
- What is the heart of an owner?
- What is the heart of a father?
- *Whose heart must first be turned, the heart of a father or the heart of a son? Unturned hearts:* limit the appearing of the Lord in our churches; *limit the establishing of proper relationship*; allow the curse of immaturity on our ministries.
- *Have we through our conversation and attitude injured the child the Lord would bring through our church?* Zacharias was promised a son from the angel. His unbelief would have killed this possibility. God had to stop

his speech so that he, in his ignorance and unbelief, would not curse the promise of God. Does the Lord at times need to do similar things to us?

- Like Elijah, do we know how to properly train our ministry sons?
- John the Baptist had the heart of a father that said, "He must increase but I must decrease." Is our heart for the increasing of Jesus through sons if it means our decrease?

Lesson Five: The Place of Circumcision in Father/Son Relationships

Him would Paul have to go forth with him; and took and circumcised him because of the Jews which were in those quarters: for they knew all that his father was a Greek.[6]

Every father must circumcise his son. It is a necessary part of the process of entering into ministerial relationship with a father. Unlike the above example of Timothy, circumcision from a father is not a physical cutting away of flesh but a spiritual cutting away of offense. Circumcision involves pain. In Timothy's case of being a young adult, it also involved a certain amount of embarrassment. It was a real test of submission. A ministry father must cut off the flesh of sons.

God will not overlook his order to fulfill His will as evidenced by His willingness to kill Moses for failure to circumcise his sons. Moses' calling would have been limited by his lack of willingness to follow the order of God and likewise our ministries will be limited if we fail to follow proper order with our sons. Spiritual circumcision involves a process of cutting away those attitudes and expressions in the flesh that hinder spiritual and ministerial growth in sons.

Circumcision by fathers is not making a list of undesirable aspects of our sons and then proceeding in some haphazard way of performing spiritual surgery. Rather, it is the act of patiently and carefully sharing truth for the removal of offense and the growth of the son. It should not be an act of abuse but an act of love. Often it is done without conscious knowledge on the father's part, but rather some action or plan of a father may bring forth a response on the part of a son that demonstrates what is happening.

Remember circumcision is not castration. One speaks of a more productive life, the other of destruction of son's ability to produce. Only religious and immature spirits seek to castrate sons so that only one man or a religious organization can be the source of production in ministry.

Ministry Checklist

- In what way has our ministry father circumcised us?
- If the cutting of our fleshly desires and carnality by a true father causes us to reject the father, are we legitimate or illegitimate sons?
- Can you have a covenant without cutting?
- Are we willing to circumcise sons even if it brings unintended offense?
- Do we know how to perform spiritual circumcision using a knife of love and not abuse?

Lesson Six: We Must Hear Our Father's Voice

And the Father Himself, which hath sent Me, hath borne witness of Me. Ye have neither heard His voice at any time, nor seen His shape.[7]

The voice of a true father is necessary for a son's entrance into ministry in higher dimensions. We must be called, chosen, and faithful in ministry. Many have a call from God but that does not give them a right to begin ministry. Between the calling and the choosing is a strenuous preparation so that the son can come into complete purpose. Only God can call us, but only a true ministry father can choose us for service and only we have the ability to be found faithful in the work.

Called saints who enter ministry before a father's choosing or enter through the sanction of religious systems will suffer attributes of premature ministry. Even Jesus did not enter ministry until He heard the voice of His Father. When we enter ministry without the choosing from a true father, we put at jeopardy the possibility of our ministries ever becoming generational. Proper father/son order is predicated upon both fathers and sons hearing the voice of God. We must be able to hear the voice of God over the shouts of men. Religious people didn't understand who Jesus was because they couldn't hear the voice of the Father.

Ministry Checklist

- Are we listening to the voice of a father or a religious voice? Do we know the difference?
- Are we teaching our sons to follow the voice of God or our voice?
- Do our sons understand what a proceeding word is? Do they understand it as our word or the word of God through us?
- A religious voice may speak to us telling us it is our father—are our sons able to distinguish such voices?

Lesson Seven: The Requirement of Wilderness Experiences

And thou shalt remember all the way which the Lord thy God led thee these forty years in the wilderness, to humble thee, and to prove thee, to know what was in thine heart, whether thou wouldest keep His commandments, or no.[8]

The wilderness is a place of emptiness and separation. God is always bringing true leaders out of the wilderness. It is a place of preparation for service. Even Jesus was led into the desert to be tried and readied for ministry. "It is the process of the wilderness that heightens our desire for growth and intensifies our desire to be filled." Immediately after He heard the voice of the Father, Jesus was led into the wilderness. Sons should be taught to expect and to allow the wilderness to make them ready for ministry.

Ministry Checklist

- Have we taught sons to expect and grow through wilderness experiences?
- How do we know we are submitted to our ministry father?
- Is it possible for a son to grow to the place where he will be able to receive inheritance without going through the wilderness?
- Wilderness experiences shape our identity and purpose. Can we write a statement of our identity and purpose for our son's instruction?

Lesson Eight: Ordered Generations—Not Gifting—Is the Sign of Successful Ministry

These are the generations of Noah: Noah was a just man and perfect in his generations, and Noah walked with God.[9]

Generation is the ability to pass on or generate in a continuous manner. Legitimate ministry should desire the generation of its vision and the passing down of its inheritance. Did you ever think that Noah was not called by God to build the ark because he was a great carpenter or a mighty preacher? Besides being a just man, Noah was *"perfect in his generations."* God knew Noah would pass on righteousness through his generations just like He knew Abraham would command his household and children.

For all his other abilities, this seems to stand out the most when looking at Noah as a minister able to fulfill the vision of God. Of what purpose would the flood have been if Noah would not have had any descendants with a heart after God? The lasting effect of great spiritual leaders is not their gifting but their ministry that continues in the ministries of others.

Ministry Checklist

- How many generations can we identify at present?
- How do we know that what has been passed on to sons will be passed on to others as well?
- What is the purpose of each generation?

Lesson Nine: We Need Our Father's and *The* Father's Anointing

And the holy garments of Aaron shall be his sons' after him, to be anointed therein, and to be consecrated in them. And that son that is priest in his stead shall put them on seven days, when he cometh into the tabernacle of the congregation to minister in the holy place.[10]

Everything should grow through the generations, yet the Church unfortunately, has not. After 2,000 years we have not experienced the power and extent of spiritual influence of the early Church. By now we should be many times beyond it, but we have not grown in the order of father and sons. Not much of our father's anointing and ministry carries on to us and even less through us.

God desires His Spirit to flow and increase in His people. The Word foretells of the Spirit being poured out on all flesh and the Spirit being within His people as a river of life. The anointing of the Spirit in ministry is part of father/son order. Just as the garments of Aaron became the garments of his son, so we need the anointing contained in our father's garments.

Ministry Checklist

- Are we in order with our ministry father so that what flows down to us may continue on to our sons?
- We all have an anointing, but have we educated our sons in stirring up the anointing?
- Submission is at the hem of the garment where the greatest anointing is. Have we instructed our sons in positioning themselves for anointing?
- Does the presence of anointing alone qualify a minister to govern?
- Can anointing be in a son's life who is not in proper order?

Lesson Ten: The Importance of Relationship

And He goeth up into a mountain, and calleth unto Him whom He would: and they came unto Him. And He ordained twelve, that they should be with Him, and that He might send them forth to preach, and to have power to heal sicknesses, and to cast out devils.[11]

More than anything else, the Lord's purpose for us can be summed up in His desire for relationship. He loves us. The Bible is not just a book to learn about Jesus but a writing that can bring us into relationship with the Almighty. In ministry we have to desire more than power or positive effect. We need to desire relationship. Our church bodies need to be connected as families and not just gatherings of people in association.

False fathers seek honor and submission that is not their right because they have no true relationship with sons but only association. Their desire is more for what the son can do for them or the value of the son to promote the father's ministry, than it is for the son and his spiritual welfare. The ability to develop genuine relationships is the key to establishing father/son order.

Ministry Checklist

- *True fathers desire to raise sons with inheritance who are able to reproduce vision and purpose. False fathers desire obtaining servants to rule.* Jesus had a plan to invest His ministry in sons. Do we have a plan that will put our ministries into our sons?
- Do our ministry sons speak and promote our vision above personal considerations?
- Do we as fathers have the bond of the Spirit with our sons?

Lesson Eleven: Honor Is Central to Relationship

Honour thy father and thy mother: that thy days may be long upon the land which the Lord thy God giveth thee.[12]

Giving honor is central to all right relationships. Our lives begin in relationship with our parents. It is a relationship not of our choosing; it was solely their choice. Yet it is from this relationship that most are to receive their greatest instruction and training in the issues of life. God makes giving honor in this relationship one of the Ten Commandments. Honor is administered in various ways to a father. It can be verbal. More significant forms of honor are submission, financial, care for needs, work in the father's ministry, support for father in face of opposition, and loyalty.

Ministry Checklist

- Sons learn by example. Do we expect honor from sons that we are unwilling to give our father?

- Giving honor to a father is a commandment with promise. How is the amount of various kinds of honor indicated in our ministries?

ENDNOTES

1. Isaiah 3:4-5.
2. 1 Corinthians 4:15.
3. 1 Samuel 2:35.
4. Deuteronomy 30:5.
5. 1 Kings 8:17-18.
6. Acts 16:3.
7. John 5:37.
8. Deuteronomy 8:2.
9. Genesis 6:9.
10. Exodus 29:29-30.
11. Mark 3:13-15.
12. Exodus 20:12.

CONCLUSION

*T*his *book*, along with the book *You Have Not Many Fathers* and their related workbooks, provide in-depth instruction into understanding and applying father/son order. The application of these materials will change forever the traditional concepts of ministry. Adopting this biblical ministry order will free and empower ministry as well as provide a means for pastor and saint alike to walk in their full purpose and find their God-given destiny. It is my sincere prayer that these materials not only provide important information but also biblical foundation to bring ministries and churches into Kingdom order.